Dear Maureen & I

With love

for your

ORLA'S CANVAS

Constant support

&

encouragement,

Mary

ORLA'S CANVAS

by

Mary Donnarumma Sharnick

www.penmorepress.com

Orlas Canvas by Mary Donnarumma Sharnick

ISBN-13: 978-1-942756-20-0(Paperback)
ISBN 978-1-942756-21-7 (e-book)

BISAC Subject Headings:
DRA001000DRAMA / American / General
FIC000000FICTION / General
FIC043000FICTION / Coming of Age

Editing: Chris Paige
Cover Illustration by Christine Horner

Address all correspondence to:

Michael James
Penmore Press LLC
920 N Javelina Pl
Tucson AZ 85748

"I found I could say things with color and shapes that I couldn't say any other way—things I had no words for."

Georgia O'Keeffe

DEDICATION

For Donna Maria Padula—
Cousin, Mentor, Friend
December 26, 1944 – January 31, 2015

PART ONE

Chapter One

Holy Week was so humid it took from Holy Thursday till after services on Good Friday for Mamma's present to dry. Easter morning, Miss Cruz hadn't even started singing *"Allons les Citoyens"* to her cats in the alley back of our house when I hopped out of bed and took the card from under my pillow where I knew it'd be safe.

I held the painting out the length of my arms and blew on it once. Then, satisfied the colors had set like I wanted, I tiptoed down the stairs to Mamma's bedroom. I hoped she was still asleep.

Outside the street was quiet. Our beagle Harper crisscrossed the road where it merged into Main Street, sniffing for some live thing to eat. It was too early for the seven o'clock bells to be ringing at St. Marguerite's. A vase full of last week's palms stood tall on the little table by the front door, and I smiled at the yellow, almost green of the fronds that curved like ballerinas' arms.

I yawned and rolled my neck around my shoulders. Felt my caramel hair curling in the damp. Looked down at my toenails turned bubble-gum pink from Mamma's polish she let me borrow.

1

The fronds stared back at me, same as people do, like they're waiting for something to happen. Or brushes, some small as pussy willows, others big like pony tails about to swish, when they motion to me, "Come on." Give me some parchment, empty as a field at planting time, or smaller papers like windowpanes, and I'm ready to fill them with shapes and shadows, motion and light. Like I'm answering the colors back, "Okay, let's go."

I sneezed and the palm fronds shivered. Mamma's mattress squeaked.

"Orla?" she said.

Her voice was two notes rising.

I went into her room, the painting behind my back.

"Happy Easter, Mamma."

Mamma rolled toward me from the big bed where my Daddy used to sleep, too.

"For me?" she asked, wiping sleep sand out her eyes. The lace on her nightgown was unraveling. She'd tied a little knot so it would stay.

She looked at the card a long time, opening one section after the other.

"Why, you've painted the trees along the river," she said.

The Chartres River ran right through town, "which is southeast," Tad always said, "until it catches up with the Mississippi and joins it on to the Gulf of Mexico."

Tad's here so much he most feels like my brother. Already won a full scholarship to the Jesuit high school in New Orleans straight from the seventh grade. I'll sure miss him every day come September, but not havin' to listen to him read me some fact every time one excites him will just give me more time to paint.

In my picture, trees hung over the moving water like they were canopies. Willows, soft pines, some with Spanish moss

2

draped like lacy spider webs. If I listened hard at night, I could hear them moving, making brushing sounds, saying, "Hush, now, hush."

A rabbit peeked out from behind each tree I painted. Sometimes he was on all fours. Other times he stood up and looked around. In the last painting, he stared down at an Easter basket with five eggs, each one a different pastel. I tried to get the colors soft as the down on my next-door-neighbor Lizzy's chicks.

"Well, thank you, Orla," Mamma said. "And I've got something for you."

She stepped out of bed, pulled on my Daddy's robe from the war hospital, and went over to her wedding chest. She opened the lid and lifted out a dress, not all flouncy like a little girl's, just two ruffles that fluttered from the wide straps that crossed in the back.

"Do you like it?" she asked. "I used the white eyelet Mrs. Haldecott gave me, and I've been keeping the ribbons in my sewing box for years."

I put the dress right on. Two buttons looked like pink roses attached the straps in the front, and pink and peppermint-green ribbons criss-crossed my waist. Mamma tied a bow looked like streamers in back. The pink ribbon matched the lining, so I didn't even need a slip.

"Mamma," I whispered. "When did you make it?"

"While you were sleeping the past few nights. After all, I want you to look pretty at the Egg Hunt."

Mamma got out of bed and stretched. Sometimes she looked as smooth and long as a model in a magazine where the writing said, "Use some powder today. You'll be glad you did."

By the time the church bells started ringing, we were ready to fetch Lizzy and her mamma. Lizzy's daddy died

3

most a year ago. Struck by lightning, just like that. Half orphans, Lizzy and me. Like having a tear so big in my dress pocket that my fingers kept feelin' round the hole. Difference was Lizzy remembered her daddy. Only way I know mine is from the wedding picture in my treasure box, with Mamma in the dress she sewed from Mrs. Taylor's formal parlor sheers. My Daddy looks uncomfortable, with a big bow tie scrunching his neck and the suit Grammie made him wear to the church. Part I like best is he's holding Mamma's hand and she's looking down at it.

I don't remember what he smelled like, or how he carried me, if he ate his gumbo spicy, or whether he could sing. Most of my life, it's been just Mamma and me, 'cepting for when Grammie Gleason, my Daddy's mamma, came to help. She quit her laundry job over to Fortner's Plantation to live with us till I started school so Mamma could work for Mrs. Castleberry full time. Soon's I got to first grade she sailed back to her brothers in Ireland so she could "die on the old sod." Still makes me sad just thinking of her. Taught me Hail Mary, and Glory Be. I wear the cross she gave me on a silver chain around my neck, even in the tub.

The four of us walked first to St. Marguerite's, where I got to light a candle for my Daddy, then the mile to the Castleberry house down river. Mamma wore a navy blue picture hat Mrs. Haldecott gave her. She tilted it so it most covered one of her eyebrows. Her gloves had little pearl buttons at the wrist. When I wanted to play with them once, she told me no.

"They're special," she said. "You can wear them to your first formal dance like I did."

I held her hand so I could feel how soft they were. Smooth and cool and cotton white.

Soon as we could see Mrs. Castleberry's house, Mamma started telling Mrs. Crowther that when she was a child, Old Doctor Castleberry ran the clinic right out of the place, with Mrs. Castleberry bein' the nurse.

"Sick as a body might be, Eloise," she said, "a person always felt like she was going for a visit."

Mamma pulled at each glove to make them smoother.

"Unless Old Doctor Castleberry had to do a medical procedure requiring him to wear white, he always wore a suit coat and a bow tie. Even when I was a little girl, he would bow ever so slightly and say, 'Well, now, welcome, young lady. What seems to be bothering you today?'"

The picture of Old Doctor Castleberry over the fireplace in his library had him in a tuxedo. His hair looked like maple syrup.

Beep, beep.

A horn honked behind us and Tad hopped out of his daddy's red convertible that looked like it had fins growing out the back. Mr. Charbonneau tipped his hat and drove slow beside us so he could talk to Mamma and Mrs. Crowther. He and Tad were dressed the same, with striped ties and blue blazers. Tad would be havin' to dress like that every day come September.

"Happy Easter, Ladies," Mr. Charbonneau said. "Addie's home preparing Fern Mae's basket of goodies. We'll be stopping down to Convent to see her while Tad helps Mrs. Castleberry get rid of her pies. Could I trouble you to make sure he leaves some for the other guests?"

Tad scrunched up his shoulders at his daddy and passed a half-empty basket of his mamma's brownies to Mrs. Crowther and Lizzy.

Mamma held onto her hat to lean toward the car. We stood behind her.

"You say hello to Fern Mae for me, Stan," she said. "You tell her I think of her whenever I make popovers."

Mr. Charbonneau looked into the car mirror to make sure no one was behind him.

"Will do, Minerva. Thank you. See you in church, Eloise."

He looked behind him once more, tipped his hat again, and said, "Bye, son, you have a good time."

Lizzy wiped chocolate off her mouth with the back of her hand as he drove away.

"Oh, Lizzy," Mrs. Crowther said.

She pulled a handkerchief out of her pocketbook.

Lizzy rolled her eyes, then asked, "Who's Fern Mae?"

Tad was eating another brownie.

"My aunt," he said, offering me the basket.

I shook my head and said, "I'm waiting for the candy."

I bent to shake some dust out of my shoe, then looked up at Lizzy. "She's the girl in the picture I painted, the one I showed you at school."

Lizzy watched me smooth my dress.

"The one who got beat up?" she asked.

Mamma looked over at us, her eyes wide open.

"Why, I didn't know you even remembered Fern Mae," she said.

Mamma turned to Tad.

"The only time I ever heard Old Doctor Castleberry sound stern, in fact, was when your Aunt Fern Mae got hurt," she said.

Lizzy came closer to Mamma to hear. "What happened?" she asked.

Mamma cleared her throat.

"Well, Fern Mae had a tough time being born and didn't get enough oxygen. She had trouble figuring out the difference between a person who would treat her right and one who wouldn't."

Tad kicked the dirt with his right shoe.

"She's retarded," he said. "She thinks everybody's good."

We walked together, Mamma and Mrs. Crowther in front, the three of us right behind.

"One evening," Mamma told Mrs. Crowther, "when Fern Mae was just about to turn nineteen, she was on her way home from Sam's Fish Shack when some fellows from Baton Rouge pulled on by her in a car. One thing led to another, and ..."

"They got her pregnant," Tad said.

His voice was like a boulder hitting the ground.

Lizzy's face turned red and she stared at her hands.

"When her condition became clear," Mamma said, "Old Doctor Castleberry advised she stay with the nuns. That's where you and your mother go every Sunday, right, Tad?"

Tad nodded, then looked to the basket, deciding against another brownie.

"What happened to the baby?" asked Lizzy. She stopped walking to listen.

"He was adopted by a family that couldn't have a baby of their own," Tad said. He rubbed the back of his head like he always did when he was uncomfortable.

"Doesn't Miss Fern Mae miss him?" I asked.

Tad rubbed his head again.

"I don't believe she ever saw him," he said. "That's what my father told me. She didn't even have the chance to give him a name before the adopting family came for him."

I couldn't imagine not seeing my own baby.

"Look," said Lizzy, and pointed straight ahead.

A line of children was filing through the picket fence that surrounded the Castleberry yard. Mrs. Castleberry stood at the gate, greeting everyone. She was small and old, but right lively, like Sam's terrier. She wore her white hair in a bun on her neck, "a chignon," Mamma told me to call it.

"Mrs. Castleberry is of French origin," Mamma said. "Her maiden name was Dubois, 'of the woods,' and her first name, Bellefleur, means 'pretty flower.'"

"Pretty flower of the woods," I said out loud.

"My name is boring," said Lizzy.

"Why, you're named after your grandmother, and she was named after a queen!" said Mrs. Crowther.

"Oh," said Lizzy, then ran ahead to where the Castleberry fence began.

We caught up.

"Hope I have some room for Mrs. Castleberry's desserts," Tad said. He rubbed his stomach and ran his tongue around his teeth to wipe away the chocolate.

Mrs. Castleberry motioned us to come in. She patted her neck with a lace handkerchief.

Tad looked down into the basket his mamma had sent and said, "The brownies were meant for you, Mrs. Castleberry. But I seemed to have tested too many."

Mrs. Castleberry laughed and laughed. She took the remaining brownie and bit into it. Little chocolate crumbs fell onto the path. She put the rest of the brownie back, then took the basket and put it on the ground beside her. When she stood up, she shook her head left and right.

"Oh, bother," she said, and fanned herself with her handkerchief.

Mamma stepped in front of Tad. "Are you alright?" she asked.

Mrs. Castleberry waved Mamma away. "Of course I am, Minerva."

She sounded like she was shooing her cat out the yard. Mamma walked past her, white gloves clenched either side of her Easter dress.

"Tell your mother the brownies were delicious, Tad," she said.

"Oh, Minerva," she called to Mamma, this time in a pleasant voice, "before I forget, I have some books for you, so don't leave without them."

Mamma didn't answer.

Mrs. Castleberry's been lending Mamma books since Mamma was in high school. Mamma reads more than anyone else I know. When we go to the library every Friday afternoon, she lingers after I pick the six books I'm allowed. She's read most everything in the place.

"If it weren't for Mrs. Castleberry," Miss Dexter, the librarian, told me, "St. Suplice would've run out of books for your mamma long ago."

"Wow," said Lizzy to Mrs. Castleberry, "you painted your house."

"Yes, indeed," smiled Mrs. Castleberry. "I decided to do a bit of research and had the house re-painted as it was originally, before my late husband subdued it to white."

The house looked like an Easter egg. Mamma said it was a Queen Anne cottage. Lizzy counted five colors. The wood slats looked like just-cooked shrimp, the shutters palm leaves, egg-nog trim around the windows, dark green doors, and white railings with designs in the other colors around the veranda to match the picket fence. Our house looked like a doll house compared to it, only without the colors. Plain grey 'cepting for the "Welcome" sign I painted pink. Mamma hung it on the front door.

ORLA'S CANVAS

"Mothers, help yourselves to some punch," said Mrs. Castleberry. "And young ladies, find four eggs each and you'll win a prize."

Lizzy and I made for the potted ferns on the veranda. They were always filled with eggs, and the little kids' arms were too short to reach all the way inside. In no time we were ready to collect our prizes.

Mrs. Castleberry greeted some more people on the path. One was a Negro man wearing a navy-blue striped suit and a white collar looked like the kind our priest, Father Carriere, wore. He had a little boy in short white pants with him whose bow tie was choking his neck. The boy kept pulling it away from his collar, twisting his neck like we did in gym class to relax our muscles. First I thought the man was one of Mrs. Castleberry's musicians or a waiter who had no place to leave his boy, but when Mrs. Castleberry handed him a plate of tea sandwiches herself, I knew he and the little boy were company. I'd never seen Negro guests at Mrs. Castleberry's before. Everyone was staring at the two of them, but Mrs. Castleberry and the man acted like they didn't notice. She just sat down at one of the card tables covered in a lace tablecloth, then the man and the boy did the same. The man's black shoes were so shiny the sun bounced off them. The little boy's feet didn't reach the ground, and he moved them back and forth like he was on one of the park swings. He studied his hands. Finally Mrs. Castleberry motioned for Lizzy and me to come sit by them.

"Reverend Makepeace, these young ladies are Orla and Lizzy. I'm sure they'll be happy to introduce your Spencer to Tad, who will help him find some treasures."

Reverend Makepeace stood up and bowed to Lizzy and me. I nodded back, the way I always saw Mrs. Castleberry do. Spencer hopped off his chair.

10

"What treasures?" he asked. He made bird-flying motions with his hands.

We waved over to Tad, who slid pieces of lemon meringue pie into his mouth while he walked toward us.

"Would you like some pie, too?" Tad asked Spencer. "It's delicious, Mrs. Castleberry."

Mrs. Castleberry smiled up at him.

"You've got meringue on your cheek," I mouthed the words from my chair.

I handed him one of the napkins I had ironed for Mrs. Castleberry yesterday afternoon. Tad patted his face, then refolded the napkin and put it down onto the table.

Spencer nodded and looked up at Tad, leaning his neck all the way back. His bow-tie wobbled.

"Chocolate pie," he said.

His daddy laughed. Tad put his plate down onto the table and shook hands with Reverend Makepeace.

"Go ahead, son," said the reverend.

"I like chocolate pie, too," said Tad. "Chocolate cream."

While Tad led Spencer toward the buffet, Lizzy and I walked to the prize table just up the path toward the kitchen door, where we could choose between chocolate bunnies or peppermints. Mrs. Castleberry always spent the afternoon before her party filling pastel-colored bags with green-and-white-colored peppermints. After that, she lined up two-inch tall chocolate bunnies on silver trays, then covered them with aluminum foil overnight. All of a sudden we heard a fuss.

Man's voice growled, "... leaving now, I say."

A boy answered, sounding scared, "Stop, Dad, No!"

Slap! like a bat cracking.

I dropped my bag of candy, grabbed Lizzy, and said, "Let's go watch."

11

We ran down the path and saw Kathleen Cowles crying, her left cheek bright as watermelon. Her daddy, Mr. Cowles, whose own face looked like boiled shrimp, was pulling her away from the party towards the fence. Her arm had finger marks on it above the elbow.

Denny Cowles yelled, "Let her go, Dad. You're hurting her."

Mr. Cowles let go Katie's arm, then grabbed Denny's so tight Denny couldn't get away. The shirt his mamma had probably ironed the night before was getting all wrinkled from Mr. Cowles's grabbing and pulling. The right sleeve looked like an accordion.

"Let me go!" he yelled.

His father shook him like a throw rug or a Raggedy Andy doll.

Lizzy covered her eyes. I walked closer, hoping Mr. Cowles would let go if he saw me. But he didn't look my way, not even when I clomped my shoes on the path.

"Let me go, you bastard!"

"I'll show you who's a bastard," hollered Mr. Cowles. He let go his son's arm, took a step back, then punched Denny's arm so hard Denny fell down.

Katie kicked her father's ankle. When he went to grab her, old Mr. Patrick, who'd been passing deviled eggs on one of Mrs. Castleberry's silver trays, let the whole thing drop. Sounded like a muffled gong.

Mr. Patrick got between Mr. Cowles and his children. Mr. and Mrs. Carroll rushed over from their lawn chairs to help. Mrs. Carroll took Katie in her arms while Mr. Carroll grabbed Mr. Cowles' arms tight. Hard as he tried to hold on, Mr. Cowles tried to get loose. Took Mr. Smith and Mr. Herne, Mr. Patrick's son-in-law, who had once wrestled an alligator down in Key West, to keep Mr. Cowles from attacking his own children.

"Jesus, Jimmy, relax," said Mr. Carroll. "We'll let you go. Just relax."

Mrs. Castleberry stood up from her chair and shaded her eyes. I pretended not to hear Mamma call from the veranda.

"Orla, come here right now. Right now, I say, young lady."

Mr. Patrick spoke in a voice sounded like God.

"Mr. Cowles, what is the trouble here that would make you hurt your own children? Calm yourself, sir. There'll be no violence here."

Mrs. Castleberry started over while Reverend Makepeace hurried to the buffet where Spencer was eating pie with Tad.

Mr. Cowles stood glaring into Mr. Patrick's face like it was a mirror and he needed to find something stuck in his eye.

"Who do you think you are to tell me what to do with my own children?"

He stared hard. Then he looked over to Mrs. Castleberry and hollered, "No children of mine will eat candy with niggers!"

Everybody stopped moving. All I heard was air. Mamma and Mrs. Crowther rushed down from the veranda and marched over to Lizzy and me, holding onto us like we'd fly away if they let go.

Mr. Carroll and Mr. Herne, still holding onto him, pushed Mr. Cowles backwards toward the fence and the road.

"Jesus," I heard Mr. Carroll, say, right into Mr. Cowles' right ear, "Jesus, Jimmy, I don't like niggers any more'n you do, but it's the old dame's party, so just shut up and take your kids home."

13

Mr. Carroll pushed as he talked, with Mr. Herne doin' the same. Finally they got Mr. Cowles out the yard and onto the road. The children followed behind. Katie was sniffling and Denny studied the ground.

"We'll see everybody home safe," said Mr. Herne, loud enough for Mrs. Castleberry to hear.

"Stop your crying, Kathleen," I could hear Mr. Cowles say from the other side of the fence by the lilac bushes, "before I give you something big to cry about."

Then, just like she hadn't noticed a thing, Mrs. Castleberry called over to Reverend Makepeace, who had his arm around Spencer, "Why don't you and I go inside where I can show you my husband's war commendations, Reverend. Tad is quite the historian, so he can show Spencer pictures from the European Front."

"Yes, Ma'am, that's a good idea," said the reverend.

He, Tad, and Spencer started for the house ahead of Mrs. Castleberry, who stretched her arms out behind them just like the mother duck did her wings in the storybook Mrs. Castleberry gave the littlest children every Easter.

Blessed Easter Greetings, Bellefleur Castleberry, she inscribed every time.

Mamma motioned for me to go over and help Mrs. Carroll, who was on her knees picking up the ruined deviled eggs. Already ants were crawling all over the yolks Mamma had mashed and seasoned yesterday. Twelve dozen eggs in all.

People started leaving right away, pretending it was really time to go. Mamma, Mrs. Crowther, Lizzy, Tad, and I helped Mr. Patrick put the lawn furniture in place. Mrs. Carroll's new yellow dress had grass stains round about her knees.

"My husband will see that Jimmy calms down," she said. "I can't think how his wife copes. I imagine she had to cook down to the hospital today. One of the loveliest women I know. Poor thing."

I wondered if Mr. Cowles talked to his wife the way he did to Mrs. Castleberry. I couldn't believe anybody'd use a tone like that with her, even if they didn't like Negroes.

Sometimes, though, I hear Mamma mutter things about Mrs. Castleberry. She sings "the witch is dead" song from *The Wizard of Oz* every time Mrs. Castleberry criticizes her for going to see the same movie more than once. Her favorite is *Splendor in the Grass*. She's seen it four times already. Cost her one week's laundry pay from Mrs. Haldecott.

Personally, Mrs. Castleberry doesn't bother me. Only thing I have to make sure to do around her is pronounce French words the way she likes. She had me illustrate place cards and menus for her company lunch last Tuesday. When I spelled out the word legumes, then said it out loud, she told me it sounded like leg-ooms.

"Be careful, dear, or you'll sound as if you are not proud of your heritage."

"But I'm not French, Mrs. Castleberry. Both my Mamma and my Daddy's people...."

But she wouldn't even let me finish.

"Hush," she had fussed, "I can't think if you continue talking."

I felt like sticking my tongue out at her. She bosses everybody around. But I just rolled it around in my mouth and thought, "Leg-ooms, leg-ooms." It was hard not to giggle. Mrs. Castleberry stared down at the place cards and alphabetized them, starting with Haldecott and ending with LeVigne. Didn't even look up when I finished and said, "Au revoir." I said it perfectly. Real slow, too.

Mrs. Carroll tossed me a bundle of napkins from the buffet table. I looked around the yard. Carrots and celery sticks made wilted streamers on the grass. There'd be plenty of laundry for Mamma tomorrow, lots of it grass-stained from when folks got all flustered from the uproar and dropped their napkins. Most the white lace tablecloths had chocolate fingerprints on them. The long linen rectangle Mr. Patrick always wore on his left arm when he served lay on the ground next to the silver tray all smeared with mashed egg yolk and paprika. I gathered up as many of the tablecloths as I could carry on one arm, making sure not to pull a tear in them when I lifted them off the tables. I made three trips into the Castleberry house to the laundry, where I dropped the soiled linens into four straw baskets Mrs. Castleberry had marked—the first for "whites," the second for "delicate whites," the third for "darks," and the last for "rags." Looked like a row of big Easter baskets gone wrong. The mess would probably get Mamma going again tomorrow like she did when I told her about Mrs. Castleberry's correcting me.

One time, just when the lilacs were about to bloom, I had come home from the Castleberry place and was using Mrs. Castleberry's pretending-to-be-polite-but-really-being-annoyed voice, the one she uses when she's telling me how to speak. Mamma started flinging our just-dried bed sheets into the basket like they were too hot to touch. I expected her usual lecture about being polite to old folks, but Mamma started bad-mouthing Mrs. Castleberry instead.

"You know everybody breathes the same air better than that old snob, Orla. I do her laundry, remember. Nobody knows Mrs. Castleberry's dirty laundry better than I do."

I wondered what was different about Mrs. Castleberry's laundry than anyone else's. But when I asked Mamma, she told me she was "using the term figuratively."

"How?" I said.

Mamma had just finished throwing the sheets and was on to the dish towels. Flung them the way firemen throw us candy at the Fourth of July parade.

"Sometimes, Orla, people say 'dirty laundry' or 'skeletons in the closet' to refer to the things they hide from others, things they don't want others to know."

She picked up the basket and motioned with her head for me to open the screen door.

"What doesn't Mrs. Castleberry want folks to know?"

I closed the door behind us and helped fold the dish towels into thirds so they became little blue squares. Mamma threw back her hair and twisted it into a bun with one of the elastic bands she wore on her wrist.

"Let's just say she's not as honest as she'd have people believe."

Mamma and I stood at either end of her double-bed sheet and folded it together across the kitchen.

"What's she lying about?"

One corner slipped out of Mamma's hand, so we had to start again.

"Plenty."

"How do you know?"

Mamma carried the sheets to the linen closet in the hall. She laid them on the shelf over the tablecloths.

"Trust me, I know."

She smoothed the sheets with both hands. They made the closet smell like fresh spring air.

"Do you have dirty laundry, Mamma?"

Mamma turned to me, closed the door, and twisted the knob until it clicked.

"Truth be told, everybody does, Orla. The trick is to keep it from blowing off your own clothesline."

She turned the basket on its side against her bedroom door and pushed me back into the kitchen toward the refrigerator.

"What are you hiding from me?"

Mamma opened the refrigerator door and smiled.

"Your lunch, smarty pants."

She took Sunday's ham and some mustard out of the refrigerator.

"Tell me, Mamma, really."

She sliced four pieces of yesterday's bread and put them in the toaster.

"Not yet."

I put my arms around her, swayed her left and right, like we were dancing.

"Tell me."

Mamma pretended to slap me. Her hand made a breeze in front of my face. Then she zipped her lips closed with her hand, pushed me away, and laughed. She stood by the toaster to wait. I punched her on her arm. Again.

"Tell me. Come on, I mean it. Tell me."

I pulled at her arms like I was shucking corn. Mamma looked at me, serious, straight into my eyes.

"No. Not until I'm ready."

I stared back. I hated her.

"Tell me!"

The toast popped. Mamma grabbed it, then dropped it hot onto our two plates. She licked her fingers cool.

"No. That's enough. Now sit down and eat lunch."

"Make me."

Mamma looked angry, stared at me hard. I stuck my tongue out, picked up my toast, and flung it into the air. Even before it landed, I knew I had gone too far.

"Orla, how dare you throw food!"

I got out the door before she could catch me and slap me for real, then raced down to the river. Even before I dipped my foot into the inky water, I knew, first chance I got, I'd steal the key to Mamma's bedroom drawer.

Now, alone after the Easter party gone wrong, I dropped the last load of linens into the already overflowing baskets and opened the cabinet where Mrs. Castleberry kept her soaps. Maybe Mamma'd need to send me for more detergent tomorrow. Then I'd have plenty of time to sneak around her bedroom at home. But there were still three bottles, each one full.

I was just about to hide two of them behind the bleaches on the top shelf when Mamma walked in with an apron.

"Quite a party, huh?" she said.

Chapter Two

Miss Foster kept letting us paint. Every day, after math and reading and geography, she'd bring us outside under the covered pavilion, and we'd sit at the picnic tables, painting in the shade. I didn't want summer to come.

I was spending most of the time imagining what to paint next. First I did shutters. A body can find plenty interesting just looking across the alley at Miss Cruz's shutters. They're wide, made of wood. Cement ledge. Birds sit there 'til they're startled. Early morning the shutters look most like mahogany, same as Mrs. Castleberry's big dining room table. By noon, caramel. Whenever I squint, seems like they curve and shimmer. At school, using oils, I painted a set of notecards with a different-looking shutter for each card. Miss Foster kept hanging them on the clothesline. After they dried, usually in two days 'cause of the damp, I put what she called my signature on the back—a little rabbit looking right out at me, my name, Orla Gwen Gleason, in cursive, all around him. Sometimes me and Mamma use them as bookmarks.

Mamma loves books. Can't live without them.

"I keep this one under the sofa," she said one day, "because it's too big for the shelf."

She 'bout crawled under the sofa Mrs. Haldecott had told us was "yours or the yard sale's, Minerva." Mamma slid the book out from an old pillowcase that kept the dust off, and she and I pushed together and made one lap. The book fit across our four legs.

"Heck, Mamma, this is heavier than Harper," I said.

"Now, the Arthurian Legend," began Mamma, sounding practically like Miss Foster when she wanted us to write down what she was saying, "was first a French story about an English king who believed people could behave well if they thought of others before themselves. King Arthur tried to do right and, let me tell you, it was a chore. His best knight, Lancelot, and his own dear wife, Guinevere, fell in love and practically ruined Camelot forever. But Arthur was not permanently discouraged. He knew people sometimes make serious mistakes."

"Were Lancelot and Guinevere sorry?" I asked.

"Not for a while," said Mamma. "But in the end, they felt bad they had hurt Arthur, so they left Camelot and went their separate ways, she to a convent, he back to France, and Arthur forgave them."

"Why'd you name me after her? I asked.

"When you were born, the little curls on top of your head looked just like Guinevere's curls in this picture."

Mamma opened to page one hundred and thirteen.

"Prout Castleberry gave me this book as a graduation present from high school," she told me.

She said his name slow, in a radio voice, like it was important.

Guinevere's curls looked like little waves. She wore a long dress and a dunce's cap, only lavender.

"Look," I said, "inside the cover looks like peacock feathers."

"Someone painted the edges of each page with gold leaf," Mamma showed me.

"Hey, there's writing on the first page," I said.

To Minerva, my own princess.
Your knight. Ever after,
Prout.

"Was he your boyfriend?" I asked.

"Long time ago," Mamma told me.

"Was my Daddy?"

"Yes."

"How'd you know which one to marry?"

Mamma lifted the book, slid it back into the pillow case, then knelt down and pushed it under the sofa. She pondered a bit, took her hair in both hands and held it top of her head. Then she sighed.

"My mother told me," she said. "My mother knew which one, Orla Gwen."

Chapter Three

Every Memorial Day, St. Marguerite's Catholic Church held its annual carnival and craft fair. Mamma and I planned to bake red, white, and blue cupcakes and blueberry pies. Lizzy's mamma was in charge of corn on the cob. Mrs. Castleberry ran the whole thing. This year, her sister Yvette was visiting all the way from New York City, and Mamma said, "The fair has to be even better than usual."

Miss Yvette worked in a museum. Mamma said she was a docent, showing visitors all around, especially French ones, since she spoke the language just the same as English. Seemed like everybody thought Miss Yvette was a lot smarter than them. All I know, she wore high heels all the time, even when Mrs. Haldecott invited her over for cocktails in the gazebo. Miss Yvette just slipped off her high heels and walked down the hill barefoot. Her toe-nails were shocking pink. I know 'cause Mrs. Haldecott asked me to serve the hors d'oeuvres.

Mamma told me not to talk to anyone, just answer if they spoke to me. That, and stand up straight.

Miss Foster was there, too, telling about how she was going up to New York during the summer and see some plays. On my way up the hill to get a tray of shrimp, I heard her tell Miss Yvette, "I believe she has some talent."

I know Miss Foster and Miss Yvette were talking about me 'cause their eyes were still watching me after I closed the screen door, "Quietly, quietly," like Mamma had told me to, and I turned around to look back.

In school the week before the fair, Miss Foster had said, "Students, I have an announcement. As you know, St. Marguerite's fair will be held next Monday, Memorial Day. Mrs. Castleberry, the coordinator of the event, has asked me to tell you that she would like to display the art work you have been making in this class. We have five more days to get ready, so be prepared to paint and draw every day."

We all clapped. This meant no more word problems.

Chapter Four

"Too bad Tad never had the chance to meet your Daddy," Mamma said while we were putting food dye into the frosting for our cupcakes. "Your Daddy was part of history, being in the war and all."

Tad likes history the way I like paint. He knows that St. Suplice should really be St. Sulpice, but somebody switched the letters on the land deed and, "There you have it, Orla, we've been living in a misspelled town ever since."

Any time a soldier or sailor comes through, Tad wants to talk with him about the war. He saves all kinds of magazine articles about battles in a peach crate in his bedroom. He's all excited because Lizzy's uncle's going to come to the fair, since his ship's docked in New Orleans and he's got liberty.

My Daddy joined the Army right after he graduated high school in 1942. He was a mechanic, and Mamma told me again, like she always did, "That man could fix any kind of machine. And build things. My, he tinkered with pieces of wood until, before you knew it, they became stools and beds and curio cabinets. He always had work, and folks sure did miss him when he went into the Service."

We separated the frosting into three bowls.

"Grammie was scared when he caught that shrapnel in his right arm," Mamma said, "that his fixing days were over. But the doctors tended to his arm just fine. It was scarred, all right, and the skin never got smooth-feeling again, but it worked just like it used to. So when he was shipped back from France to the Thayer Hospital in Nashville, he exercised hard and, by the time he got back here, even before he married me, he was able go right back to work in Hank's Garage."

I heard Tad come up the steps. Mamma had asked him to bring along his red wagon so we might load our sweets trays onto it. I looked out the window by the chair I always sat in for supper. There it was, bright as a fire truck, a small American flag tied with black twine around its handle.

"Are you and Orla about ready, Ma'am?" he asked Mamma.

"Don't you look ready for a sporting afternoon," Mamma said.

Tad held a baseball glove in one hand and carried a badminton set in the other.

The three of us put all the baked goods onto a tablecloth we folded into Tad's wagon and walked down to the center of town to St. Marguerite's.

Most everybody White in St. Suplice came to the fair. A body could spend the whole day just eating and playing games. Most the time, the old folks set themselves fanning under the awning with a big sign next to it saying, Awning Courtesy of Charette's Hardware and Supplies. The mothers got bossed around by Mrs. Charbonneau, Tad's mamma, who giggled after nearly everything she said, so nobody

26

minded. She assigned them to the different food stands, where their faces got redder and redder by the hour. Mr. Carroll led the daddies refereeing ball games over to the park back of the church. There was gumbo and po' boys and cotton candy and corn; beignets, pies, cupcakes, and crepes; iced tea, lemonade, soda, apple-berry punch; a popcorn machine, two ice cream makers, and pickles in wooden barrels.

Ladies from the retirement home on Hester's Ridge held parasols while white-capped nurses pushed them in their wheelchairs. Baby girls in their strollers wore cotton bonnets. Father Carriere wore short sleeves and sunglasses. He was showin' Reverend Makepeace around the property with Mrs. Castleberry, who was wearing a dress with little tulips all over it, walkin' from person to person, saying, "Thank you for making such a splendid fair. Won't you say hello to Reverend Makepeace. He's been working with Archbishop Rummel to open our school to all children next September."

Mrs. Castleberry waved me over to take a plate of beignets into the rectory. Then she led the reverend to Mr. Herne who ran Bingo every Friday evening. He was sitting with some others in the shade just outside Father Carriere's study.

Mr. Herne rolled his eyes at the organist, Mr. Brochu, after they shook hands with the reverend. Mr. Brochu's face turned red. Then he went to re-arranging the chairs he had already put into a circle front of the bandstand.

You'd better wash your hands now, Mr. Herne," laughed old Mrs. Allaire.

She sat on a folding chair by the bandstand with two pillows that let her be high enough to see over the card table in front of her. She wiped her eyeglasses with a hanky and adjusted her straw hat.

Mr. Herne laughed back.

"I guess our fair is being in-te-gra-ted, Ma'am."

He talked like Mrs. Allaire was deaf. Made sure Mrs. Castleberry, Father, and Reverend Makepeace heard him too. But they just kept walking.

"Not just the fair, Mr. Herne," she said.

She tried to sit up tall from her pillows, but the folding chair wobbled.

"They're fixing to integrate the school. My son told me Father Carriere sent a letter from the archbishop to the parents a few weeks ago. Can you imagine?"

She re-arranged her ceramic figures on the table by type: a row of cows, another of piglets, a third of lambs.

"Do you think my son will let that priest sit our Elise next to some nigger boy itching to get his hands on her? He'd sooner send her to public school. Told me he'll drive her down to Convent to the public one there if he has to."

I wondered if anybody else would leave our little Catholic school when the Negroes came. How many kids could the school down at Convent hold, anyway? Only reason I can stay in St. Marguerite's is Mamma does Father Carriere's sewing and mending. And we're White.

Mrs. Allaire pulled on her blouse. Her neck was turning red.

"Afternoon, Mrs. Allaire," I said, crossing over to the rectory.

I hoped she didn't want to talk to me. Didn't know if I should tell her not to say "nigger" or respect her 'cause she was old.

"Orla," she waved. "Have you heard from your lovely grandma in Ireland?" she asked.

I kept walking.

"Yes, Ma'am," I looked back, "just last week. She's enjoying the spring, she said. The warmer weather makes her arthritis feel better. Thank you for asking."

I didn't know what to think. Mrs. Allaire seemed nice to me. Grammie used to knit baby blankets for the orphanage with her. Spencer Makepeace acted too polite to hurt Elise. And it was White boys anyway who raped Fern Mae. When Mamma told me what that meant, I could hardly stand knowing it.

I walked up the rectory steps and pushed open the big oak door. It felt cool inside, dark as a cave, most all the curtains drawn against the sun. I went into the kitchen that smelled like coffee and blinked to get used to the dark. I put the beignet dish in the center of the table next to the napkin holder. Right there on the green-checked tablecloth was the morning paper, with two photographs that caught my eye. One was of Archbishop Rummel in his miter. That's what Mrs. Castleberry told me his headpiece was called when he visited for Confirmation last May. The other was of him again, with two regular priests, a nun, and Mrs. Castleberry. I squinted to see the words underneath: "Archdiocesan Commission members Rev. Edwin Coffey, S. J., Rev. David Dwyer, Sister Madeleine Marie, R. U., and Mrs. Bellefleur Castleberry face stiff opposition as they plan to integrate New Orleans' parochial schools."

I didn't know why somebody Mamma said was so snobby would choose to help Negroes. Maybe you had to be Mrs. Castleberry to do such a thing, since wasn't anybody ever argued with her to her face. Can't imagine Mrs. Allaire phoning her to complain. Mrs. Castleberry even told Father Carriere what to do. One time he had to change the Mass schedule because it conflicted with her garden show.

"It's a small thing to ask, don't you think, Father?" she had said.

I know 'cause I was serving them tea. Mrs. Castleberry had made it sound like a question. Father Carriere didn't answer, just kept sipping from his cup. Then the next week in church, he told the rest of us.

"As it benefits the Seton Orphanage," he announced from the pulpit, "we can all celebrate the Eucharist one hour earlier next week."

I heard the band warming up outside. Some of the instruments sounded like big cows lowing or a bird trilling.

I wondered how I'd like bein' as powerful as Mrs. Castleberry, if it was fun or just made other folks talk about you behind your back. Took another look at the paper, put it down the same way I found it, then took my time getting back to the door and out into the sun.

The church bells were chiming eleven o'clock, and I looked around for Lizzy. I couldn't find her. I did see Miss Yvette arrive in the Haldecott's car, though, and first thing she did was walk right over to Miss Foster. My teacher was sitting in a lawn chair right between two shade trees on the edge of the church park, wearing a straw hat and sunglasses. Tied from one trunk to th'other were all our paintings. Miss Yvette and Miss Foster walked along talking, Miss Yvette asking lots of questions and Miss Foster nodding and pointing to the pictures.

I was on my second strawberry ice cream cone of the afternoon when Miss Foster came on over to me.

"Good afternoon, Orla," she said. "Miss Yvette would like to speak with you and your mother about your art work."

Mamma left the pie and cupcake stand to Mrs. Cowles, took off her apron, and said, "I won't be long, Bridget."

30

Miss Yvette surely did ask lots of questions. Did I enjoy painting? How did I get the idea for the notecards with the shutters? Had I ever worked with charcoal?

"It's fun," I told her. "I like to tell stories with the colors."

"Tell me this one," she said, holding my painting of Miss Fern Mae by the river.

"I bet Miss Fern Mae felt scared," I told her. "That's why her eyes are closed. I bet she was afraid to look. So I took the sunshine out the picture, 'cause she prob'ly saw dark."

"Why do you have some light up here in the corner?" Miss Yvette asked.

"Don't rightly know, Ma'am," I answered. Prob'ly 'cause she didn't end up dying by the river."

"And this one?" Miss Yvette pointed to a tree dripping with Spanish moss like the one I'd painted for Mamma.

"That tree is always reachin' over the water, kinda like it wants to keep the river from rushing away. A body can see it from Mrs. Haldecott's kitchen window, right over the sink."

Tad and Lizzy ran over, all out of breath.

"Come on, right now, Orla! Water balloon toss is about to start."

"May I be excused, Miss Foster?" I asked.

Miss Yvette answered for her.

"You go ahead, young lady, I want to speak with your mother."

Chapter Five

Mr. Herne had surrounded the parking lot with the large orange cones workmen used to block off danger zones on the state roads. They looked like ice cream cones dipped in marmalade glaze.

We all lined up, two rows each, facing one another—Lizzy across from me, Denny from Tad, the smaller kids, Dotty Herne and Katie Cowles, and the ten-year-old Dobson twins from Inez, come to visit their cousins, the Carroll's. Anyone didn't reach Tad's elbows got to stand closer to his teammate, "to compensate for their shorter stature," Father Carriere said.

Lizzy tossed first and I caught the red balloon, which felt plump with water. Tad and I had been practicing all week with an old pair of rubber gloves used to belong to Mr. Frick, who traded them with Tad when Tad helped him write a letter to the tax collector. The gloves dripped some since we had only string to tie the wrist parts, but they worked pretty well, anyway.

"Let the glove or the balloon fall into your hands," Tad said. "Hold your hands together, like they were a bridge, so the balloon will rest there without breaking."

I did like he said, and Lizzy's balloon rocked on my hand bridge, feeling like somebody's heart pulsing right onto my fingers.

Tad and Denny did fine, too, for three rounds, till Tad lost his balance on a mound of pebbles, tripped, and splashed the balloon onto the pavement.

"Sorry, Denny," he said.

Denny shrugged his shoulders, and they both sat down between two cones.

Little Dotty Herne threw her purple balloon too short so it never even reached Katie Cowles, but went splat on the ground.

Katie was already sniveling when Mr. Herne handed her a yellow balloon and said, "Whyn't you give this one a try."

Nobody appeared to mind he was letting Katie cheat.

Pretty soon it was my turn again.

"Throw it hard," said Lizzy.

She was bouncing up and down like a basketball.

"Now!" I flung the balloon.

Lizzy caught it, grinned, then yelped like a puppy as water drenched her face.

"What happened?" I asked, and ran over to see.

She wiped her face with her hands and took a rubber band from her wrist to pull her hair back into a pony tail.

"I guess I should have taken off this birthstone ring I won at darts. It must have punctured the balloon."

Sure enough, one the prongs on the ring stuck out, lookin' like a tiny television antenna.

We joined Denny and Tad between the cones and watched the Dobson twins, who hadn't dropped one balloon yet, become the winners.

Father Carriere held up their arms like they were prizefighters and said loud enough for everyone down at the food stands to hear, "Ladies and Gentlemen, Boys and Girls, I declare Mark and Anna Rae Dobson, direct from Inez, Louisiana, the winners!"

Everybody clapped and Mrs. Carroll brought out two identical green inner tubes with black letters on them said, A Gift from Carroll's Sundries. She put the tubes over Mark's and Anna Rae's heads. Time they walked over to Minnie Herne to have their picture taken with Mrs. Castleberry for next year's church calendar, the tubes had slipped down to their waists and brother and sister looked like two ballet dancers in tutus.

"Nice dress, Mark," said Denny.

Mark stuck his tongue out at Denny, pulled the tube up to his shoulders, and pretended he could fly.

Tad and I began collecting the cones so Mr. Herne could take them back to his friend at the state transportation office. Looked like we were carrying orange towers on each hand. We piled them up behind the ambulance and the sheriff's car, where nobody'd bother with them. Sheriff Powell and Mr. Squires, the ambulance driver who took my Daddy down to Convent just before he died, were leaning against the ambulance smoking.

"Orla, Tad," Mr. Squires said.

His white shirt had a red cross on the pocket, but underneath you could see a tee shirt with Dixie Boy in cursive.

Sheriff Powell winked at me like he always did.

We nodded, trying not to lose our balance. Mr. Squires blew curls of smoke out his mouth. He dropped his cigarette stub and ground it into the dirt with a boot pointy as a steak knife. He turned and watched us pile the cones into columns of four. As we came around again, the police radio sputtered out from the sheriff's car like grease crackling on a grill. Sheriff Powell leaned in to pick it up. Tad and I looked at each other and knew to take our time so we could hear what was goin' on. Was like we were in each other's head. Tad knelt down to tighten his sneaker laces, making a double knot on each one. I shaded my eyes and pretended to watch the baseball game over in the field.

"By Sam's Fish Shack, you say? Over." the sheriff said.

Tad stood up, walked closer to the field and watched, too.

Mr. Squires lit another cigarette.

The radio sputtered again. Sheriff Powell took off his hat, ran his hand across his forehead, put his hat back on, then answered, "I'll be there shortly. Over."

He pulled his head out from the police car.

"Let's go get some food," Tad said.

"Okay."

I made like I was walking on a tight rope, one foot careful in front of the other, with my arms out wide at my sides.

"Anybody looking for me, I'll be back soon as I can," Sheriff Powell said to Mr. Squires. "Some dog got run over by Sam's place. He's splattered all over the road and one of the Desmarais biddies in the duplex across the way is having a conniption."

Didn't seem interesting enough to stay, 'cept I wondered whose dog it was.

"Heads for gumbo," I yelled, and flipped a nickel from my pocket.

"Tails, shrimp!" said Tad.

Time we dumped all the shell leavings into the trash, the band was ready for the afternoon performance. Father Carriere was announcing each number with the bullhorn he used every year, and most of the old folks were already seated close together around the bandstand. They reminded me of wagon trains lined up for the night. Mrs. Allaire sat right in front of the podium. Mrs. Castleberry settled down between her and Reverend Makepeace. She turned to talk to Mrs. Allaire, but Mrs. Allaire just nodded and stared straight ahead like she was hypnotized by the band. Reverend Makepeace fanned himself with a program.

Once the music started was when the ladies who did all the cooking took a break. One after another they lifted their aprons up to wipe their faces and Mrs. Charbonneau brought them iced tea or beer, whichever they liked, compliments of Father Carriere. The teams came in from the fields, plopping down on the chairs and benches scattered around, and Mr. Carroll handed out po' boys to the referees "to re-energize you, men," he said. They ate fast, gulped down their drinks, and soon Mr. Fenn and Mr. Kipp fell asleep right in their seats, both their heads dropping to their chests like ripe fruit from a tree.

"Mamma," I called, and ran to sit by her at the dessert stand. It was a pink-striped tent with a table now just half-full of peach and blueberry pies, coconut cookies, angel food cake, and decorated petits fours. Mamma sat on a low bench in front, legs stretched in front of her, her shoes and apron off to the side. Her cheeks looked like Raggedy Ann's.

She was taking the last bite of her hot dog and drank her beer in six gulps. She licked the mustard off her fingers. Near where Miss Foster had been sitting, Tad's grandpa and a couple of his neighbors were playing cards. Tad pulled a folding chair up to the table they'd made with plywood

36

across two police horses and they dealt him in. Two babies crawled around on some blankets spread out one next to the other on the grass, and a third one, Carol Ann Howell, just eight months old, was rocking almost asleep in her mamma's arms.

This was my favorite part of the fair. St. Suplice became a mural of most everyone I knew—old folks like Mrs. Allaire by the bandstand tapping their feet or their canes, Tad's mamma and daddy at the soda fountain sipping cool drinks and chewing food they'd worked at all morning, babies gooey with ice cream, high school boys and the girls who giggled at them as they strutted across the field, men in straw hats who talked baseball and politics while they shuffled cards and bragged about fish they had caught. Everybody tired from having too much fun, the sound of Mr. Charette's trumpet and Mr. Howell's horn reminding us we were still, though barely, awake.

Mamma and I swayed back and forth to the music, the horn's melody unfolding across the church grounds like a tablecloth ironed perfectly smooth.

"When I fall in love, it will be forever...."

"Forever," Mamma sang along, pretending to hold a microphone.

She stood on the bench and moved her hips to the song, bent her knees and curved her body all the way around like a dancer onstage. Brought her free hand to her lips and blew a pretend kiss to an audience that wasn't there.

Mrs. Carroll and Mrs. Charbonneau applauded.

"Crooning, Orla," Mamma said. "Your mother's a star, and she's crooning."

The ladies laughed so hard they had to wipe their eyes.

I had to love my Mamma then.

Chapter Six

Just as the applause was dyin' down from "Sister Susie's Sewing Shirts for Soldiers," Miss Yvette and Miss Foster were making their way from the shade trees up toward the bandstand nearer the church. Miss Yvette's silver bangles jingled on her wrist in time to the click of her heels on the blacktop. Miss Foster wore sunglasses and a scarf around her hair just like Mrs. Kennedy.

"The two of them could be in a fashion magazine," Mamma said, like she was reading my mind.

She had finished her number and was layin' the length of the bench on her side. She wiggled her toes every now and then.

All of a sudden a roar of engines down the road drowned out the next song. Then again, this time louder, two different roars and the squeal of tires going from stopped to real fast quick as a darting fox.

Way beyond sense for a churchyard full of folks, a green pickup and the livery jeep Mr. Cowles drove for his second job zoomed through the two stone pillars into the parking lot. Miss Yvette and Miss Foster ran separate ways to get out of the way, Miss Yvette to the left side of the yard, Miss Foster to the right. They shaded their eyes to see what was going on.

"Hey!" Miss Foster shouted, "We have children here."

"You're not in charge here, teacher lady," a man's voice barked.

The truck driver laughed a loud laugh that wasn't funny. Looked to be Bob Twomey, who worked in a bar down in Convent. He kept honking the horn like it was stuck. Folks gathered round him at first, seeing what he'd come for, then one by one backed away, hurrying their children out of sight. The music stopped at the commotion and people in the audience turned from a group into moving parts, Mrs. Allaire grabbing her pillows to her chest, Mémère Adele looking this way and that, Mr. and Mrs. LeVigne first standing, then sitting, then standing again, not knowing where to go, like ants when you sprayed them with poison.

Mr. Twomey flung a dirty rag that landed on Miss Foster's face. She yanked it off and threw it back, but it fell short. Mr. Twomey laughed some more and raced the engine. Threw a beer can out the window hit her right in the chest. Miss Foster jumped, then backed toward the trees. She wiped her face with her arm.

"Here's some excitement for you, nigger lovers!" he yelled in a voice sounded like an angry dog.

A bottle flew out the car.

Crash, whoosh, then black smoke, and a stink like rotten eggs. Another from the livery jeep. More from the green truck. Glass shattered over the parking lot.

Somebody yelled, "Fireworks!" and got some cheers.

But Mr. Carroll and Mr. Fenn shook their heads no. They pointed quick to everyone by the stands and motioned us to head toward the church.

"Hurry now," Mr. Carroll said to his daughter. "Do as I say."

When the smoke cleared, Miss Yvette had disappeared.

The Fayette's and the Beaulieu's ran to their cars parked side by side, Mrs. Beaulieu using her skirt like a cape over her two boys, not caring that her slip showed. Tad and the other card-players took their plywood table cover, hurried over to the blankets, and held it in front of the mothers and their babies.

"Stay down," I could hear Tad tell them. "Just stay down."

Carol Ann woke up. Her cries sounded like a lamb bleating. My own heart beat hard.

"Mamma," I clutched her dress.

She was quiet, biting her lip, the way she does just before she tells me what to do.

"Into the church, into the church," Father Carriere bellowed into the bullhorn.

A swarm of bodies jostled each other going up the stairs, some into the main entrance, others the side door near the rectory.

Mamma grabbed my arm, pulled my face to her, and said, "We're going to run, Orla. Run across to Tad, then around the back way to the rectory and into the church. We get separated, you keep running. Do you hear me? Do not let those men see you. No matter what they say, do not go near them."

I blinked to stop the tears.

"Fern Mae," I mouthed, tasting her name on my lips.

The rifle shot up. A blast, a whooooosh, then wings. Birds screeched and "danger, danger" rang in my head.

"Inside!" I heard Father again, and across the way folks were moving like Mamma said we were going to.

Tad's daddy prodded his wife, who didn't want to go without him, but he kept nodding to her, saying she must. Mr. Carroll helped Signe St. John with her walker.

The man standing in the back of the green truck shot the sky again. My shoulders twitched at the blast. I looked at him hard to make sure what I saw was true. He was M. J. Kane, one of the meat-cutters over to Phelps' Grocery. He gave me a slice of cheese whenever I picked up Mrs. Castleberry's order.

"How are you today, darlin' girl?" he always asked.

I wept, couldn't believe it was him. I felt like a fool.

"Liar," I screamed in my head, "you rotten, stinking liar!"

Everyone was moving. Like the tidal wave in the movie about Japan Miss Foster had shown us, each person took another's arm, winding and rolling toward the church.

When the wave got in front of us, Mamma and I raced behind it past home plate and around toward Father Carriere's study. We crouched panting under the louvred windows. Most everybody was gone, either already inside or kneeling beneath the windows in their cars. Mr. Carroll bolted the side door by the vestry after he lifted Mrs. Allaire up the last step. The ambulance stood where it always did, only I didn't see Mr. Squires. Across the way, Miss Yvette's face poked out over a hedgerow, but only for a moment.

It was too quiet. Even the horn had stopped. Birds swooped into the yard like dive bombers to peck at food dropped in a hurry, their necks twitching, their eyes darting around like mine. Mr. Charbonneau came behind Mamma and me, patted Mamma on the back, then slipped into the bandstand from the side. He squatted and walked low by the stage to near Reverend Makepeace's chair.

ORLA'S CANVAS

I tried to breathe slowly, one breath at a time. Mamma rubbed my shoulders. Father Carriere, Mrs. Castleberry, Reverend Makepeace, and Mr. Charbonneau all stood up against the stage, the instruments spread out on the floor behind them. Looked like a receiving line, with Father still holding the megaphone.

"Shhh," Mamma pulled my head toward her and put her finger to her lips. "Don't make a sound," she whispered.

I nodded slowly. Breathed deep.

Mr. Twomey opened the door and swung out from the driver's seat of the green truck. M. J. Kane jumped over the side with his rifle. He aimed it toward the bandstand. My muscles grabbed, my throat closed. Mamma held me by both arms. Mr. Cowles stepped out from the jeep said Owens' Livery: We Make Your Destination Ours. He went around the back to the door opened sideways, where he always packed the Haldecott's luggage when he chauffeured them to their hunting lodge. Just as he did, two more men, Mr. Thomas, who passed the basket at Mass on Sunday, and Mr. Fellowes, who made specialty shoes in his garage, got out, too. They must've been lyin' down hiding before. Each one had his hand on a pistol at his waist. Mr. Cowles picked up a baseball bat.

Father Carriere walked toward them slow, like he did when he went from row to row in church, asking us catechism questions on First Fridays.

"Now I know you men don't really want to be disturbing a church picnic, scaring people with your guns and your stink bombs. You're all people who've supported St. Marguerite's."

His voice was soft, pleasant even. Like he was talking to folks who might not understand him at first.

Mr. Fellowes and Mr. Thomas took their guns out from their holsters. I gasped and Mamma put her hand over my

42

mouth. They came close to Father Carriere and pointed the guns at his belly.

"Shut up, nigger lover," Mr. Thomas said.

Tad's daddy walked forward then, his hands up in front of him, and stood next to the priest. Mr. Fellowes nodded to Mr. Thomas, who turned his pistol on Mr. Charbonneau. Father's right arm twitched. He clenched and unclenched his fist. Mr. Charbonneau kept his hands up.

Mr. Cowles was dressed up in his chauffeur clothes, back from the airport like his wife said he'd be, when she said he'd be coming late to the fair. I wondered where she was, Katie and Denny, too, if they'd seen him or gone into church before they knew.

"We don't want to disturb anyone but the nigger," Mr. Cowles said.

He pointed the bat at Reverend Makepeace. ·Mrs. Castleberry took the reverend's arm. The reverend didn't budge.

"It's the nigger disturbing the fair. St. Marguerite's been doing just fine without niggers long as I know."

Mr. Cowles swung the bat at the air like the boys did at batting practice. Lifted his chauffeur cap up and back on his head. Stared at the minister.

I pinched the skin on my arms to keep quiet. White, pinch, hurt, let go. White, pinch, hurt, let go. I felt ashamed of my skin.

Mr. Cowles looked from Father Carriere to Mrs. Castleberry.

"And it's your fault," he said. "We thought you were plain uppity. Now you're getting yourself involved with uppity niggers, too, ruining the town."

Mrs. Castleberry stood still like the mayor's wife when he made speeches.

"And you a foreigner besides. Whyn't you go back where you came from?"

Mrs. Castleberry's shoulders got straight and she held herself tall. Mr. Cowles moved sideways from her, leaving just a few inches between himself and the reverend. He held his bat with both hands, so it made a railing between them.

"We're going to go for a ride, nigger," he said.

Reverend Makepeace looked like a statue. Mamma gripped my arms. Like a big burlap sack dropped on top of me, I felt tired, tired and sorry for Reverend Makepeace, for Fern Mae, for anybody else ever got hurt on purpose. I bit my lip. Hoped it'd bleed.

"You like socializing with high society," Mr. Cowles inched closer to Reverend Makepeace so the bat touched both their bellies. "So I'm going to take you for a ride in a high society ve-hi-cle."

He let the bat drop from one hand, then twirled it in the other like it was a harmless thing, an umbrella or a baton.

"You'll do no such thing," said Mrs. Castleberry, and she stepped right between Reverend Makepeace and Mr. Cowles.

I held my breath. Mrs. Castleberry looked very small.

Mr. Cowles shoved her so hard she knocked Reverend Makepeace back onto the stage as she fell to the ground. Her breath caught and she made a little sound, like a puppy or a sack of peaches dropping. Quick, Reverend Makepeace reached to pick her up, but Mr. Cowles swung the bat at the back of his head so hard that when he tried to stand straight, he wobbled some, then fell down, too. Blood gushed over his back.

Mr. Charbonneau and Father Carriere went to help them both, but the men with the pistols stopped them. They grabbed Reverend Makepeace and dragged him away from the bandstand.

My fingers were stuffed in my mouth.

M. J. Kane pointed his rifle at Father and Mr. Charbonneau as he backed away, too. Mr. Fellowes and Mr. Thomas spit on the reverend's face.

"They'll kill him," Mamma whispered. "Dear God, they'll kill him!"

That's when I screamed.

"Help, help me!" I cried.

"No!" Mamma shouted, and slapped my face.

The men, 'cepting Mr. Kane, ran to see what was the matter. Their guns so close to my face helped me throw up. I puked right on them. I held my stomach, fell on the ground moaning.

"Help me," Mamma said, "Help me bring her to the ambulance."

I went limp. They lifted me up, carried me by the front of the bandstand. I retched again. Water ran down my legs.

"Jesus," Mr. Fellowes said, "I'm covered with puke," and M. J. Kane turned his head to look.

In a flash, Father Carriere tripped him and Mr. Charbonneau grabbed the rifle. He pointed it at M. J. Kane.

The men dropped me and drew their pistols again. I tasted grass. Mamma threw herself on top of me.

"Shit," Mr. Thomas said.

"God have mercy on my soul, I'll use it," said Mr. Charbonneau.

Father got Mrs. Castleberry and the reverend to their feet. They hung onto his arms the way you see survivors from a plane crash do on the news. They moved towards the church in slow motion. Mrs. Castleberry's dress was stained with dirt, and the reverend's blood streamed down his back.

Mr. Cowles glared at Mr. Fellowes and Mr. Thomas.

"You've got guns," he said. "What are you waiting for?"

45

Mr. Fellowes and Mr. Thomas looked at one another.

"Cold-blooded murder," said Mr. Charbonneau. He held the rifle steady.

"Think of your families, men, think what will become of them."

He sounded calm, like when he talked to Mamma about her will.

"You in jail, me trying to work up a reasonable defense for you. It's not worth it. Too much to risk. You can never be sure of the jury."

Mr. Cowles snorted and scratched his privates. Mr. Fellowes looked at him, then back at Mr. Charbonneau, and finally put his pistol back into his holster.

"You want to kill the old lady and the priest, you go ahead," he said to Mr. Cowles.

Then he turned to Mr. Thomas and M. J. Kane, "There'll be other picnics."

Said it just like that. I bit my fingers till they hurt.

The men started back to the green truck. Mr. Cowles looked down at Mamma and me and kicked dirt at us. He walked with his bat to the lawn in front of the church. By the time Mamma and I found our way up the steps and got somebody to unbolt the door, we heard him smashing the glass on the sign that said, Church of St. Marguerite— Welcome.

Chapter Seven

"Let's clean you up," Mamma said, and she took me into the vestry.

She made me take off my clothes, then washed me from the sink like she did when I was a baby. I couldn't tell what was soap and water and what was Mamma and me cryin' all over each other. She had me wrapped in an altar cloth till she found a white cassock in a closet and dressed me. Even laughed a little at how I looked. She knelt before me and stroked my cheeks. I smelled clean.

"You shouldn't have," she said. "You might have been killed. I might have lost you."

Her voice caught and I started crying again, thinking how hard Mr. Cowles had shoved Mrs. Castleberry, not knowing if Reverend Makepeace would be alright. That I'd choke on any piece of cheese M. J. Kane tried to feed me.

The side door opened. It was Tad, his grandpa, and the other men bringing in Carol Ann and her mamma. They were white as ghosts. Carol Ann hiccupped. Right behind them came Miss Yvette covered in leaves.

She looked into the vestry.

"Thank you, Orla," was all she said.

I stared at her. Then she helped Mamma and me back down into the main church.

Looked like a makeshift hospital. Mrs. Castleberry was layin' on one pew covered in an altar cloth, holding her rosary beads. Reverend Makepeace was sitting by her, leaning forward, his face in his hands, one of Father Carriere's vestments ripped to make a tourniquet round his head. Everybody else sat in pews pretty much by family, like they did most every Sunday. Seemed folks just wanted to breathe together in a place we knew by heart. Mr. Squires went over and murmured to Mrs. Castleberry. He was just makin' to go out the door to get the stretcher for her when we heard roaring again.

"Let us pray the rosary," Father Carriere said, and Mamma and I got down on our knees.

Father's voice prayed—"Glory be to the Father, and the Son, and the Holy Ghost...."

Mamma held me close. Something outside exploded. My head felt big with noise. She kept saying the prayers.

"...as it was in the beginning, is now, and ever shall be,...."

A rock flew through the window above us.

"Mercy," yelled Mrs. Allaire.

The Holy Women by Jesus' Tomb cracked into bits of colored hail. Stained glass rained down.

"Ow," screamed Mrs. Carroll, as a long shard pierced her head.

She fell into her pew.

"Everyone get down!" yelled Father Carriere.

Mamma pushed me under our pew, then crawled over to Mrs. Carroll. I looked sideways out my left eye and saw Mrs. Cowles take off her apron and knot it around Mrs. Carroll's head. Mamma reached up her hand for somebody's picture hat and fanned it over them.

Mrs. Carroll's hair was turning scarlet, and a red stream inched like a long worm over the marble floor. Reverend Makepeace moaned.

Father's voice kept steady, "Hail Mary, full of Grace, the Lord is with Thee...."

Denny was lying on his side on the floor a few rows in front of me. I could see him holding Katie tight. He rocked her in his arms.

Something big hit the wall outside the altar dedicated to St. Marguerite. Mrs. Allaire was crying softly. Glass shattered on the roof, quick and sharp as lightning strikes. I watched for the ceiling to fall.

Father kept praying.

"Holy Mary, Mother of God...."

Smoke seeped through the windows. Squeals like fireworks before they turned into bursts of color. The hum of voices praying, praying. Then a siren coming near. I closed my eyes and covered my ears. Sounded like thunder even then.

"World without end," Father prayed.

"Amen," I heard my voice, small from under the pew.

But the siren didn't stop.

I crawled out and climbed onto the seat. My feet felt the wood smooth and sure beneath me. I faced the altar.

"Amen," I said again, like answering questions at school.

People stared.

I raised up my arms. Sleeves like white bells.

"Amen!" I bawled, "Amen!"

Out the corner of my eye I saw Mamma rushing toward me, her face like when Grammie had stepped onto the ship.

I turned to Him. Stared at the Cross. Waited.

49

"Where are you?" I cried.

If He heard me, He didn't let on.

Mamma caught me as I fell, and Mr. and Mrs. Charbonneau took us both in their arms.

Chapter Eight

Father Carriere was finishing the Glorious Mysteries when Sheriff Powell came inside the front door, marched right down the aisle.

"You got people hurt in here?" he asked, but we didn't need to tell him.

"Jesus Christ," he said when he saw me.

He went over to check on Mrs. Castleberry and Mrs. Carroll. Mr. Squires and Mr. Fenn went out to get the stretchers.

Mrs. Cowles helped Mrs. Carroll to her feet. She had blood all over her dress.

Reverend Makepeace opened his eyes and tried to keep his head up.

"I'm sorry," he said to her. Then to everybody else, "I'm sorry."

Nobody said a word.

Mrs. Castleberry said, "No, I'm the one responsible. It's all my fault."

She didn't look bossy, or even proper. Just sad, wrinkled and sad. She shook her head no at the stretcher, took Reverend Makepeace by the arm and they went outside together. They walked like an old married couple.

"You'll take us both home now, Sheriff Powell," she said. "First Reverend Makepeace, so I can speak with his wife."

The Charbonneau's, Mamma, and I followed them, Miss Yvette's heels clicking behind us, her hand on my back. The hallway was dark, so I had to blink twice when I walked out into the sun.

"Oh, no!" I heard my voice, and my hands flew up to my mouth quick as a trap door.

Looked like somebody'd gone and emptied all of St. Suplice into a giant heap of garbage.

"Jesus, Lord," said Tad. "It looks like a battlefield."

Smoke dirtied the air where the quilting booth had been. A mound of burnt fabric smoldered on the pavement and the lawn chairs were all tipped over. Chocolate, vanilla, and strawberry ice cream had turned to little streams that were drying sticky on the hot tar. Crows were peckin' at popcorn pieces scattered everywhere. The pickle barrels had rolled to a stop in the gutter just past the sidewalk, and Lizzy's dog was sniffing at the brine. Mamma's pies were smashed against the stained glass windows. Broken soda bottles cut Tad's bare feet. Corn on the cob was sticking out the statues front of the church like they were men's privates, and I felt disgusted, as if I had seen Father Carriere naked. The big awning was sliced to bits, so pieces of it hung like streamers wiltin' from the heat. Miss Foster walked around the park in her dress smelled of beer picking up remnants of treasures she could find, and Miss Yvette stood with her arms folded across her chest and said just one word: "Barbarians."

I looked past her down to where my paintings had been hanging between the shade trees. All I could see was smoke.

I ran fast as I could, tripping over my cassock. The clothesline was ripped right off the trees. The clothespins held up my pictures were broken on the ground. What was left of Miss Fern Mae's picture was curling into ash. Everything else was gone.

"Mamma!" I yelled, "Mamma!"

I screamed again and again as I circled the trees, picking up shreds of my work. Corners and edges, nothing more. My fingers felt itchy, my pulse like a hammer pounding and pounding, like somebody'd stolen a part of my heart.

Tad tried to help, but there was nothing to pick up. I felt him shaking me, taking me by the shoulders, trying to hold me still.

"Stop, Orla. You have to stop. Your paintings are gone. You'll have to paint others. That's all you can do."

I pummeled his chest and howled like a wolf in the night. Tad held me tight and let me hit him again and again. Even when my shaking turned to hiccupy sobs, he didn't let go. He held me tight even when Mamma came running. Didn't leave, just stood with us, quiet.

What made me myself had turned into dust. Disappeared into thin air like it never was. Gone. Even with Mamma and Tad beside me, I felt empty and afraid. Hollow as a tree trunk rotted.

Chapter Nine

Mamma held my hand and we watched Mr. Carroll get into the ambulance with his wife. The ambulance drove off as we walked through what had been the fair. She sat me down on the rectory steps and went down to the mess used to be her pie stand and looked for her shoes.

Mr. Cowles, still holding his bat, stood right by Sheriff Powell's car. Watched Mrs. Castleberry and Reverend Makepeace get in. Whistled.

"Go home," the sheriff told him. "Take your sorry self and your family home."

Soon as she saw her husband, Mrs. Cowles started cryin' something awful.

"Shut up," he said to her.

"You didn't," she said, like she knew but didn't want to.

She walked back towards the church. But Mr. Cowles caught her, turned her towards him, and pinched her cheeks with his fingers till he most lifted her off her feet. I couldn't even move.

"Shut up and get the kids."

I tried to get invisible, shivered, thinking what it must be like to live with him.

Tad came up from sayin' good-bye to his granddaddy and asked real soft, "Walk home with me?"

But I shook my head and went to be close to Mamma. We walked around picking up pieces of colored glass used to be The Holy Women. Tried to fit them together like a puzzle, but they were just too chipped.

"Ow," said Mamma, when one the pieces pierced her palm. "Dammit."

She peered into the cut. She didn't look pretty anymore. Her hair was stringy with sweat and she was squinting so hard two lines creased between her eyes looking like the sides of a capital H.

"It doesn't look like there's any more glass there," she said.

The blood made lines on her hand looked like roads on a map. She spit into her hand and clenched her fist to stop the bleeding.

I bent down again to find more, but Mamma said, "Don't. You'll get cut, too. Besides, it's going to take more than the two of us to clean up this mess."

I looked around. Mamma was right. Was going to take the mayor's men and Father Carriere's helpers workin' together to set everything right. But the fair could never be the same again.

Mamma flopped down on the church steps and sucked on her hand. Didn't even bother crossing her legs ladylike. I watched ants march over the melted vanilla ice cream already gone gooey in the sun. Like paint too thick. Between us, we couldn't fix a thing.

Mamma sighed. Sounded like her breath dropped right down to her feet.

"Orla," she said, and she rubbed my hair with her good hand like when I was a little girl.

When Mrs. Cowles came back out the church with Denny and Katie, none of them spoke. They all three held hands and looked at the ground as they stepped up into the back seat of the livery jeep. Mr. Cowles slammed the door after them. I could see the bat sticking out the front window on the passenger side.

I was angry enough at Mr. Cowles for hurting Mrs. Castleberry and Reverend Makepeace, for wrecking the fair, and for ruining my paintings, I could have kicked him right in the face. But at least he wasn't my daddy. Denny and Katie must surely be madder than me. Seemed to me that having Mr. Cowles for a daddy might be worse than having no daddy at all.

Chapter Ten

School ended with a surprise announcement—Miss Foster was fixin' to get married. She wasn't just going North to see some plays, after all, but to become Mr. Charles Deak's wife.

"I met him, you see, students," she told us, "down at Tulane University, in New Orleans, where we were studying at the time. And he's been starting his career up North."

I wondered how Miss Foster could just up and leave us.

"What does he do?" asked Tad.

"Will you miss us?" said Lizzy.

"He's a banker, and I certainly will. But you'll have a new teacher, come September, and, in no time at all, you'll be off to a new start."

Just 'bout when I got home to tell Mamma the news, I saw a special delivery truck front of the house. Mamma was holdin' a big box and smiling.

"Thank you kindly," she told the mailman.

He tipped his hat and drove away.

We took the box into the library room. Mamma got the big scissors from the knife drawer and slit the package right down the middle. The postmark read: New York City, and the return address was:

Miss Yvette Dubois,
c/o Metropolitan Museum of Art, Educational Programs
New York City.
Under the paper stuffing was a letter, typed.

Dear Miss Gleason:

The Educational Programs Department of The Metropolitan Museum of Art is pleased to commission you to paint five scenes of the summer season in St. Suplice, Louisiana. Please find enclosed the materials you will need to complete your commission. Upon receipt of your art work, the museum trustees will forward you fifty dollars, in the form of a cashier's check, as your payment.

Should you have any questions or concerns about this project, please contact the Educational Programs Department, phone number listed below. Due date is July 15. Packing directions are enclosed.

The museum looks forward to receiving your work to display in our "Promising Young Artists Collection," scheduled to open July 27, 1962.

Sincerely yours,
Yvette Dubois,
Director of Student Programs and Docent Tours

"What do you think of that, Orla?" asked Mamma.

I reached into the box. There were two kinds of paper, one rough and gray-colored, the other smooth and white. There were the charcoals Miss Yvette had asked me about at the church fair. Oil paints in little jars lined up in a wooden box, and water colors, like we had at school, too. Ten new brushes, each a different size, just for me.

"This calls for a celebration," said Mamma.

While Mamma made a batch of lemonade in the company pitcher, I got some ginger snaps out of Grammie's old cookie jar, and the two of us went out onto the veranda. We didn't fold clothes, or shuck corn, or sweep away leaves left from the last rain. Mamma and I just sat on the glider and rocked. Neither of us said a word.

Usually, after the second cookie, Mamma says, "Now, don't you go ruining your appetite for supper, young lady." But she didn't. She just twirled the ice around the glass with her finger and smiled without laughing. I thought about Miss Foster, wondered if she knew about the box and my commission. Maybe she and Miss Yvette would have cocktails in New York. Maybe Mr. Deak and she kissed. Maybe one day somebody would kiss me.

Right now, I was getting sleepy, leanin' against Mamma's shoulder, feelin' her breathe. I was Orla Gwen Gleason, with hair that looked like Guinevere's. My Mamma had had two boyfriends and was made to pick one. Miss Fern Mae would never know her baby boy. A barbarian could marry the nicest wife. Tad wants to be President of the United States. Houses can be many colors. Father Carriere has arms like regular men. My Daddy's scars did not keep him from building me a bed. Bad things happen quick as the lightning that killed Lizzy's daddy. Mrs. Castleberry is brave. Blood runs through my veins like the Chartres River does through town. St. Suplice is my home. I will not kill the spider weaving its web above me, close to the blue ceiling. I will put it into a picture, instead. My hair is curling in the damp. Mamma's eyes are closed, and we are holding hands. Down the road, folks are closing up their shops for the evening. The bells at St. Marguerite's ring five o'clock. Off on Hester's Ridge, the freight train's rumble begins.

Seems like time is standing still. But I know it's not. It's just me payin' attention. Watching and listening. Waiting. Tonight, after Mamma and me look at one of her books, I'll go on up to the sleeping porch. I'll close my eyes and try not to move. In my mind, I'll picture Spanish moss and lost babies, Daddy and Mamma's wedding, Grammie seeing her brothers again. Then, come morning, right after breakfast, even before Tad shows up, I'll reach into the box and start to paint.

Chapter Eleven

Morning of the longest day of the year, Tad and I had jobs to do. Each of us took half the veranda. Over on his side, Tad laid out one old suitcase, a rucksack, and a steamer trunk filled with my Daddy's things. Mamma'd feed him lunch and supper both, she said, if he'd organize my Daddy's belongings. When he finished that, he could arrange Mamma's books according to the Dewey Decimal System, too, like the real library. He actually gets excited about organizing other folks' things, like it's a privilege, or relaxing, even.

On my side, I stood over a foldin' table covered with last week's newspapers. I put a rock on each corner to keep the newspapers from shifting around. On top of Tuesday's paper, the left-side rock covered part of the picture of a demonstration in New Orleans. Some doctors wanted everybody, Negro and White, to use the same emergency entrance at Tulane Medical. Picture showed a White man waving a baseball bat at an old nun carrying a placard read, "We're all God's children."

I lined up my paints and took to painting the hydrangeas front of the Carroll's porch across the street. I had mixed the colors to look like mashed blueberries, robins' eggs, and new grass. In my head, though, the hydrangeas kept turning into faces of people hurt down at Tulane, tryin' to get through the doors of the emergency room, only the doors were all exploded. Doctors and nurses were running out the hospital in my mind, so nobody could get in. Couldn't tell who was Negro or White, anyhow, with the soot and blood running down all the faces. No way I could get back to the hydrangeas no how. So I mixed some purples, browns, and reds and turned the hydrangeas into faces. The mouths were crying and moaning, sad. One pair of eyes looked wide, like they were taking in something big, the way I felt when my pictures got destroyed. Another had them closed from the burning. I felt hot myself, angry, even, because I really wanted to paint hydrangeas. But I couldn't. I heard the explosions in my head, the sirens and the screaming, how a body wouldn't know what was happening, how she'd wipe the sweat off her face and see her hands all red instead and scream with blood on her hands dripping, "Mamma, Mamma!"

I wiped my face with the towel I kept around my neck for when I washed the paint off. Started painting hair, burning hair, some Negro, matted, some not.

Inside, Mamma was ironing Mrs. Haldecott's clothes she planned to take north to the Smoky Mountains for her annual "retreat to the cooler climate," where she went every summer to see her grandchildren. I heard Mamma re-fill the iron with water, then waited for the hiss-s-s the steam made before she started on the linen skirts.

Before long, quiet settled down on the three of us like a tired visitor on the rocker. Nothing but birds calling along the river, Mamma humming low other side of the screen, the rustle of Tad rummaging, the shh, shh, shh of my brush.

Pretty soon, four faces looked back at me. I took in a breath. Seemed like the man with the wide eyes was telling me, "Stop, you must make this stop!"

"Hey, Orla," said Tad.

It took me a moment to look away from the man's face. Then, like nothing had changed, I walked over to Tad's side of the veranda. He had neat piles of things divided, looked like by type. Some socks with tags still on them, army jacket folded neatly as the flag over Mr. Crowther's grave. A tower of black and white photographs. Some papers looked official, stamped in faded purple ink.

Tad handed me a picture. Looked like my Daddy after he got wounded. His right arm was all bandaged up and he was wearing the bathrobe Mamma wears now. Only thing was, the right sleeve hung loose off his shoulder, not wide enough to fit over the bandages, I guess. Only other picture of him I ever saw besides the wedding portrait with Mamma. He didn't smile in this one, either. Had a cigarette in his mouth and he was sitting on an outside bench, must've been at the hospital in Nashville.

Wish I could remember him. Didn't have a voice or a smell for me like Grammie Gleason did. If I try really hard, I can just about hear her, "This cross will protect you, now, my sweet. It was my own mother's before me."

I touched the crucifix on the chain hung between where my breasts were starting to come. She had sounded like fiddle music.

"Any more clothes?" I asked Tad.

He pointed to the opened rucksack and took out shirts and some skivvies. I took them from him, held them close to me, tried to imagine them on the man in the picture. Then I reached in myself. Something felt silky. I pulled out pajamas, color of the wine Mrs. Castleberry serves with roast beef.

"Doesn't look like army issue to me," Tad said.

I ran my hands over the fabric. Tad's face turned red. Felt like butterflies were fluttering around my stomach. I was glad when he turned away and reached into the rucksack again.

The screen door squeaked and Mamma came outside to wring out one of Mrs. Haldecott's blouses. She looked at me holding the pajamas, and her eyes flashed like lightning. She smiled, too, like she was happy.

"Why, I didn't know Sean kept these in there," she said.

She put the wet blouse down on the rocker, fanned her hands dry, then lifted the pajamas out of mine. She draped the pants over her arm, and rubbed the shirt across her cheeks like it was a washcloth and she was trying to get all the cold cream off. Then she took both pieces with her inside.

"Mamma, what are you doing?"

She didn't answer. I followed. She was already in her bedroom, folding the pajamas carefully, like they would tear if she touched them too roughly. She held them like they were a little baby, and laid them in the bottom drawer where she kept the two nice panties and bras she wore only on special occasions. The locked drawer with the scented paper. She bought one piece at the card shop every year on her birthday. Lavender. I'd pulled one out once when I was little.

"No," she had said, and slapped my hand. Hard.

I leaned on the door frame. Mamma closed the drawer, locked it, put the key on top of her dresser, and looked at me.

"Your daddy wore them on our wedding night," she said. "The only night I ever stayed in a hotel. The Monteleone in the French Quarter. A butler brought us champagne on a silver tray. And a bowl of fresh fruit."

She folded her arms across her chest so they looked like an X and closed her eyes. I looked at Mamma's face seemed to belong to someone I didn't know. Her eyelashes were long, and she was smiling with her eyes shut, her mouth open just a little. She took a long, slow breath, then another. I watched her fingers drum against her arms. Heard the clock on the bureau tick, then stop, tick, then stop, tick, then stop again. Felt like I was spying, so I tiptoed back outside. I wiped my face again with my towel. It felt rough. On the veranda, Tad was holding a piece of paper up close to his eyes to read the small print, I guess. Didn't say anything. The exploded people glared at me from my parchment. I needed to paint plums right away. Ripe, red, juicy plums.

Chapter Twelve

Yesterday, Mamma told me she, Tad and I were going to help Mrs. Castleberry get her house ready for some Italian visitors coming in August. We'd be going over at least twice a week till they arrived. Mamma was to wash and iron all the linens for the guest rooms and get the formal tablecloths and napkins ready. Tad would organize Old Doctor Castleberry's study. I would do some paintings of the house and yard to present to the orphanage as a remembrance from St. Suplice.

They'd be comin' from Fiesole, a little town overlooking Florence, where Old Doctor Castleberry had founded an orphanage with some fancy Italian lady Mrs. Castleberry called a countess, "La Contessa Beatrice D'Annunzio." The name of the orphanage was La Casa dei Bambini. Countess Beatrice, the head teacher, and the first student to be awarded the Castleberry college scholarship would be staying with Mrs. Castleberry before the student, a girl named Gabriella, went up to New York to study music at The Julliard School.

But when I woke up this morning ready to get started, something didn't feel right. My stomach didn't hurt, or anything like that. Miss Cruz's cats were mewing fine outside my window. But the house felt wrong. Mamma wasn't walking around the kitchen. Coffee, that's what it was. No coffee perking.

I shuffled down the stairs, rubbing my eyes to get used to the sun came in over the front door, and went into the kitchen. Mamma had written a note in big, red crayon letters over yesterday's newspaper:

> *Orla—*
> *Had to drop off some clothes at the Haldecott's*
> *early. Going directly to Mrs. Castleberry's house.*
> *Meet me there. Don't let the coffee spill over if you*
> *decide to make some.*
> *Love, M*

I pulled open the pantry door always stuck and got out the coffee can had just enough for four regular cups, or two if I used Grammie's mugs. I put the flame on high to get the water boiling. Looked in the icebox to see what I could eat and decided on the piece of peach pie Mrs. Haldecott had given Mamma leftover the other day. I poked my fork into the crust till the sugared peach juice oozed out and was about to take the first bite when I realized, here was my chance.

The church bells chimed eight as I walked into Mamma's bedroom. It was cooler than upstairs and the room's quiet wrapped around me like the sanctuary where Father Carriere would be starting Mass. Right there, top of her dresser doily, next to her Tabu perfume, my baby picture, and the little statue of the goddess Minerva, was the key to her bureau drawer. I picked it up and turned it one way, then another, in my hand. It felt like a long way down from the top drawer. I skimmed the key down the side of the bureau like it was someone water skiing on the river. Slipped it into the keyhole quick as I slid into bed at night. I turned it to the right, heard a click, and opened the drawer.

Mrs. Castleberry would have called the scent fragrant. Lavender lifted itself up and out in little gusts, making the air new with clean. I breathed deep, long breaths. Looked behind me to see if the curtains were drawn.

The coffee started to perk. I got up, walked back into the kitchen, and lowered the flame just in time. The morning paper slapped the step outside the front door. I ignored it on my way back to the drawer. The doorway to Mamma's room felt like a dare, a mouth wide open. I walked through.

I knelt in front of the drawer. My Daddy's silk pajamas were on top, folded like in a department store. I lifted them out and laid them on Mamma's bed already made with the pistachio chenille spread. Under them were the two lace bras —what Mamma called brassieres—and two lace underpanties she wore only for special occasions, like last New Year's Eve, when she went dancing with Lizzy's Uncle Kurt, who everybody called Captain. Then and another time when they went out to dinner with Lizzy's mamma and daddy before he died. One set was the color of eggnog, the other almost pink. It was hard to imagine Mamma polishing somebody's silver wearing these. I held the eggnog bra to my chest. Couldn't fill the cups even halfway.

Couple of cars drove by, one sort of fast, the other, slow as a hearse. Lizzy's back door slammed. Mrs. Crowther yelled up to Lizzy, "I'll be back soon as I go to the post office and the grocery."

Next there was a folded white bath towel, laid top of some things underneath. The towel had been ironed, 'cause the creases were still there. It was monogrammed, too. I picked it up and turned it so I could read the letters. The middle one was a C, embroidered in navy blue. The smaller letters either side, in a lighter shade of blue, were P and A. Looked like the ones Mrs. Castleberry used, 'cepting hers were embroidered in pink. I laid it aside my Daddy's pajamas and Mamma's fancy underthings.

The phone rang six times next door, but Lizzy didn't pick it up.

There were only a few more things in the drawer. They were dark. One was a man's swimming trunks, grape-colored, with a white line down the side of either leg. Must've been my Daddy's, too. The other was a lady's two-piece bathing suit, the bottom like a pair of shorts, with a flower pattern, green, turquoise, and purple. I lifted them up and out, arranged them across the bed like people were wearing them.

There was nothing left in the drawer. I felt a little disappointed. My coffee was probably ready and anyway I was hungry for pie.

I was folding the man's trunks to put back when, all of a sudden, I heard Tad clunking up the steps. He knocked on the door.

"In a minute," I hollered.

I heard Tad sit on the rocker. He'd likely read the paper while he waited.

I picked up the bottom half of the lady's suit and laid it in the drawer same as I found it. I was doing the same with the top part when something stared out at me from the white lining. I looked closer. It was writing. Black writing. Where one breast should go was a heart drawn in ink. Two letters in the center, *M* and *P*, then *Forever* around the heart. Where Mamma's other breast fit, *May 22, 1950*. Looked like two people must have done the printing, 'cause the letters for *Forever* were printed with curlicues, and the other letters like stick figures got turned in the curve of the bra cup. Or maybe Mamma had just been playin' with letter shapes like I do sometimes.

Tad knocked again, "You two alright in there?"

I felt wobbly. What if I mixed up the way they had been folded? I tried to answer regular-like.

"You go on, Tad. I'm not dressed yet. Mamma's already gone to Mrs. Castleberry's. I'll see you there."

The rocker squeaked when Tad got up, then moved back and forth, back and forth, slower each time.

"See you there, then," Tad said, and he clunked down the steps like a drum beating.

My heart thumped faster than it was supposed to. Why had Mamma written in her bathing suit top? Was she alone when she did? Maybe she had leaned over a dock somewhere, naked with my Daddy before they got married. Her breasts would have been hanging right there in the air, like a couple of grapefruits, only softer.

I closed my eyes. My privates tickled like when a spider web brushes your arm. I shivered. I wished I were little again and Mamma was holding me close to her on the rocker. I'd hear her heart beating regular as Mrs. Castleberry's metronome. Wouldn't even know the word breast.

Lizzy's phone rang again, and I heard her say, "Hello. No, Ma'am, but she'll be back in no time. I surely will have her call you."

Mamma and my Daddy got married May 29, 1950. My Daddy's initial should have been S, unless he didn't like Sean the way Sally Carroll doesn't like Margaret Sally, so she's Sally. Sean Patrick. Maybe he liked Patrick better. I can't ask Mamma 'cause then she'll know. Maybe I'll write Grammie.

But why would I ask her that? Maybe Mamma stole the towel 'cause it belonged to her old boyfriend Prout. Maybe she wanted to keep it and kiss his initials now and then, like she kept the princess book to hold onto even after she loved somebody else. Somebody she married.

I picked up my Daddy's pajamas again and laid them in the drawer. Fixed everything in the room just like I found it. But my fingers tingled. Felt like electricity was running through me. Like I had set myself aflame.

It was going to be hard to look at Mamma up at Mrs. Castleberry's. I didn't want her to know I had snooped, but I wanted to know if she was still in love with my Daddy and Prout Castleberry, even though she had to choose one of them. I wanted her to tell me her whole life story, not leave anything out. But what if the man in the writing wasn't my Daddy? I'd hate her, wouldn't let her tell me what to do. "Why should I," I'd say. "Why should I listen to someone like you?" She'd get really angry, maybe even slap my face, but I'd hit back. I'd punch her where the writing was. Punch her hard, right on her breast so she'd hurt.

Chapter Thirteen

Time I made sure Mamma's bedroom looked normal and put the key exactly where I had found it on her bureau, I wasn't looking forward to breakfast anymore. I went back to the kitchen and filled my mug the way I always did, but the coffee looked muddy. I moved it around in circles in the cup. Some splattered out onto the plastic tablecloth. I let it sit there, little smears of wet dirt. I sat down and speared a piece of Mrs. Haldecott's pie with my fork. But when it slid back down onto the plate, I didn't lift it again. I banged the fork on the plate till I got tired of doing the same thing over and over again, pushed the dish away, and went upstairs to get dressed.

On the sleeping porch I sat down on the bed my Daddy made me. My feet dangled like over water. I didn't care to move. My whole life I thought I knew everything about Mamma. But she was a stranger now. Like one day you looked down at your feet that were your feet your whole life, and there, just like a flower bloomed fresh, you saw a beauty mark under your right big toe never existed before. It'd be a kind of surprise, but one that made you jumpy instead of glad, since you had no idea it could happen, or even how it did. Like M. J. Kane ready to be a murderer.

I got dressed slow, like there were weights on my arms, made my way downstairs, all the while picturing Mamma in her bathing suit bottom with my Daddy and Prout Castleberry, two of them standing across from her on a big dock, both of them looking at her breasts. She was holding out a black pen in her right hand, waiting for one of them to take it. I couldn't see which one did. It was like a quiz show on television—Door Number 1 or Door Number 2. Pick the correct one and win the prize.

My lips quivered. I felt like jelly. They'd be expecting me at Mrs. Castleberry's. I wanted it to be winter, to be cold enough to wrap myself in the afghan Grammie Gleason made that fit around me two whole times. It was St. Patrick's Day green and ivory, it covered my body, a hiding place where I could bury my face and breathe in the wool, forget what I did, what I know now and wish I didn't. But when I locked the door, put the key on Grammie's chain around my neck, and made my way to the Castleberry place, it was summer just the same. My sneakers made almost-wet prints on the road in the damp. The morning felt like steam and, time I rounded the bend to the house, I could feel my hair curling around my neck. I felt just as uncomfortable inside, not knowing what I'd do when I saw Mamma.

The big front door opened wide into the foyer with just the screen door closed, so I walked right in. I heard footsteps upstairs, so I knew Mamma and Mrs. Castleberry were already busy with the linens. I figured Tad would be in the library, so I went there. Sure enough, he was surrounded by piles of paper and notebooks.

"Hey, Orla, it's about time you got here. Look at these."

Old Doctor Castleberry had at least twelve notebooks full of his war experiences. I remembered dusting them one time when Mrs. Castleberry had the bookshelves shellacked. Tad handed me one notebook after another. They were bound in leather, with dividers inside, and pockets to hold the pictures and letters.

One had nothing but newspaper clippings. We read the headlines: "Scores of Orphaned Children Wander Streets;" "Contessa Beatrice D'Annunzio Thanks Yanks;" "Castleberry Raises Fifty Grand for Italian Orphanage;" "Castleberry Estate Brings Orphans to American Colleges."

Tad laid the clippings out on the long library table. He put one on top the other, arranging them by date.

According to the Associated Press,

> *Peter Clemson Castleberry, M. D., of St. Suplice, Louisiana, and former surgeon with the 300th Mobile Army Surgical Hospital, has joined forces with the Contessa Beatrice D'Annunzio, of Fiesole, Italy, to open an orphanage for children whose parents were killed or reported as missing during the invasion of Italy. Castleberry and D'Annunzio have enlisted the support of the Poor Clares, an order of nuns originally from Assisi, ancestral home of St. Francis, to provide daily care of the children.*

I walked around the side of the big desk to read the rest. I wondered what it would be like to have Mamma missing, gone for good.

I read the next column:

> *Miss Julia Norwich, a British citizen and nanny to the Contessa's son Paolo, who died, along with his father, the Conte Carlo D'Annunzio, as a result of injuries sustained in a grenade attack of his father's*

74

car, has remained on staff at the orphanage to oversee the children's formal education.

The orphanage is housed on the first two floors of the Contessa's villa in Fiesole. Presently thirty children, ages two to thirteen, are in residence.

Bet they had their lessons right in the house.

Commenting on the arrangement, Doctor Castleberry said, "Americans can only begin to imagine the effect of war on young children. The Contessa and I thank all those who have contributed thus far to the children's cause."

Donations to La Casa dei Bambini, Fiesole, Italy, may be sent c/o The Red Cross.

In an orphanage, who would a body love?

I looked at the pictures of Prout Castleberry on his daddy's desk. In one he was in a baby carriage, with a bonnet on. Then, in another, Prout and his daddy were holding fishing rods and wearing shiny rubber boots. They were both laughing. The third, Prout's portrait, from college, I guess, had him looking away from the camera at something made him smile, but only a little.

"Is that you, Orla?" Mamma called down. "Did you make yourself some breakfast?"

She came into the library carrying a large boxed marked Office Decorations. I tried to look at her, but my eyes kept moving to her feet. She was wearing her white sneakers with the hole where her right big toe poked through.

"What's in the box?" I asked, pretending to be interested.

Mamma put it down and stretched her back. Her breasts moved up when she moved her elbows backwards.

"Just some curtains and seasonal decorations Old Doctor Castleberry had for his office. We're emptying out the storage room upstairs so we can make it a bedroom for Miss Norwich, the teacher coming from Italy."

Mamma once told me that Old Doctor Castleberry had birthed lots of babies in town, came right down to our house to help me get born. Mamma said she was supposed to go to the hospital Mrs. Cowles works at down to Convent, but "for a first baby, Orla, you came mighty fast. Even Sheriff Powell, speeding like he can, was going to be too slow for us. So Old Doctor Castleberry strode in after your Daddy ran to fetch him, took a look at the situation, and said, 'Now, Mrs. Gleason, seems like your baby doesn't want to cause you the trouble of leaving home for the hospital. Your baby wants to be born right here.'"

Then came my favorite part of the story.

"As soon as you were born, Old Doctor Castleberry held you up so I could see you. He had his operating mask on, of course, and all I could see of him were his blue eyes and his bushy red hair. 'Look, Mrs. Gleason, look Minerva, you've gone and birthed yourself the most beautiful baby girl.'"

Then Mamma told me, my Daddy and Grammie came into the bedroom to meet me for the first time. They each took a turn holding me.

"And," she said, "they laid you in my arms."

I hugged myself, imagined Mamma holding me for the first time. Wondered if the little hairs on my arms felt like down on a baby chick.

When my Daddy started for his wallet, Mamma said, "Old Doctor Castleberry told him, 'No charge, Mrs. Gleason, no charge, Sean. Since the war, seems like people are paying me when I see a baby born. God bless you all. I'll be by later to check on everybody.'"

Mamma said she and I both went to sleep then, and my Daddy went on up to the sleeping porch "so he wouldn't disturb us."

I was still tryin' to picture me and Mamma in the big bed, when Tad said, "Look, Orla, pictures."

Mamma picked up the box and said, "You two look at the pictures. I've got to get these things into the shed. Orla, when you finish, come upstairs. You can help Mrs. Castleberry and me with the bedding."

I watched Mamma walk away from behind. Her hips swayed left and right, making her housedress move like water lapping. She wore a one-piece bathing suit when we went swimming together. A maillot, she called it. Wonder if she'd have Lizzy's uncle write in it if they ever decided to go to the beach. Maybe he's already seen her breasts. Maybe she only wore her fancy brassiere so she could take it off in front of him. She'd tan my hide if I took off my clothes so Tad could see.

"Modesty is always becoming, Orla," she says.

I don't know anyone modest who'd let somebody not even her husband write in her brassiere. She's always telling me how to behave while she's probably been acting bad herself. My nipples twitched thinking what I'd feel like Tad saw me naked.

"Here," he said, and I jumped as he pointed to three pictures side by side on the desk.

Some were of children, others of a big house. The same children were in the first three pictures. Seven of them, four boys and three girls. Some had shoes and no socks. The boys wore short pants. One girl was missing an arm. Only one boy was smiling. The dresses on the girls looked raggedy. Everyone had dirty hands. On the back of each picture, someone had written, 1943.

You ask me, they looked like the three kids I saw in the *Times Picayune* last Thursday got left by the bayou not far from Lake Pontchartrain. Their own daddy just went and dropped them by the roadside with one quart of milk and a box of Rice Crispies. Girl had on a sleeveless dress looked like one of mine, with three daisies across the front. It felt kind of scary. Like looking in a dirty mirror.

Mamma came back in holding a feather duster in one hand, a chamois cloth in the other. Looked around the room like Sheriff's patrol car light, round and round, blinking.

"Has either of you seen Mrs. Castleberry's eyeglasses?"

"She had them on when we were in the shed earlier," Tad said. "I'll go take a look there."

He went out the front door and around the side of the house.

Mamma looked angry. Her lips were closed tight, pressed like she was trying to keep her words inside from getting out. Mrs. Castleberry didn't like it when Mamma swore. Last Christmastime, we were cleaning the kitchen when Mamma dropped the cake stand decorated with holly, said, "God dammit all," and Mrs. Castleberry had looked right up from the table where she was stringing cranberries and nuts, turned red as the berries herself, and said in a mean-schoolteacher voice, "Minerva, do not even think of using such profanity in this house again."

That time Mamma didn't answer, just turned her back on Mrs. Castleberry, but I heard her next wash day say, "You go ahead and hire someone else if you don't want me here. You go right ahead."

That was after Mrs. Castleberry caught Mamma reading *Screen Life* while she waited for the washing machine to finish the whites.

"I can't believe someone with your intelligence reads that trash," she said. "What kind of example is that to Orla?"

I had just come into the kitchen with the sheets from the clothesline when I heard the whole thing. I dropped the basket real hard so the two of them would stop time I got to the laundry room. Mrs. Castleberry must've heard me, 'cause she walked fast out the laundry room, nodded at me, and walked up the stairs, not quiet like she usually did, but banging each step with what Mamma called her "sensible shoes."

Soon as I heard her slam her bedroom door, I ran in to Mamma. She was on her knees pulling towels out the dryer. She flung them into one the straw baskets. Her teeth were clenched. Her mouth looked like an angry dog's.

"Mamma, why don't you just quit? Work somewhere else, where you can dress up nice and look pretty, teach school like Miss Foster?"

Every day Miss Foster matched. When she wore her blue seersucker suit, sure enough, her spectator pumps would have little blue dots somewhere on the leather. She painted her nails the same color as her lipstick. Even the clips she wore to hold her French twist in place blended with her clothes—the ivory for her lights, the horn-rimmed for rust and browns, and the black for everything else. That and she carried a briefcase. When she said, "Now, then," we all sat up straight to listen.

Mamma leaned back on her legs, took a deep breath, and looked up at me.

"Come here," she said, motioning with her sunburned arms.

I sat down on the cool tile floor beside her. She ran her fingers through my hair.

"I don't want to quit, Orla. I want you with me in this house."

I stood up, started folding the bath mats, and looked around us. Even Mrs. Castleberry's laundry room was nice, better than our place, that's for sure. Paint didn't even get a chance to peel here. Every couple of years or so, Mr. Patrick scraped down anything rough and put a new coat of lemon-meringue yellow on the walls. Floors got polished once a year, right before the Easter party. House smelled good all the time, too. Lavender in the drawers, pine smells after all the bathrooms got cleaned. And every seat was comfortable. Mrs. Castleberry wouldn't abide loose springs. Our couch had one place felt like a body's back end was getting stabbed.

"But it's not like we get to live in it, Mamma. And, besides, you hate it here."

Mamma stood up, too, grabbing all the bath towels together. She folded faster than I did. Each towel, one, two, three, made a noise like a slap when she threw it onto the counter.

"What I hate, Orla, is when Mrs. Castleberry condescends to me, when she talks down to me, as if I'm not her equal."

Slap.

I nodded.

"But she treats you differently. She knows any child of mine would have belonged in this house if I had been allowed to marry her son. As it stands, we're just the help. But pay attention and learn your French anyway. Plan to go to college or art school. Then you won't find yourself folding somebody else's laundry."

Mamma massaged her knees all red, then hugged me. I started on the dinner napkins.

"Mamma, why don't you go to college, you know, like Miss Foster did, down to Tulane?"

80

Mamma laughed, but not in a happy way.

"In these clothes!"

I threw the napkins at her. She flung them back. Started folding again.

"I'd love to, my baby, but I can't afford the tuition. Plus, how would I get there?

Tad's mamma drove. Even Mrs. Cowles. Wasn't like Mamma was too stupid. But she seemed stuck, stuck like a gatepost in cement.

"Mamma?"

She pulled the darks out of the hamper.

"Do you think Mrs. Castleberry wishes I belonged here?"

Mamma's face turned serious. She pushed the "full load" button.

"Orla Gwen," she said.

She spoke my name like a prayer, soft and slow. She put her arms around my waist and looked practically through my eyes.

"Maybe she does, maybe she doesn't. What she must know, though, is that your life would be easier if you did. My life, too. But Mrs. Castleberry wouldn't let her son marry me. And that's that."

I had to let Mamma's words sink in. Looked at the dinner napkin in my hand with the *C* embroidered on it. *A C* the color of pink sand. I imagined a Castleberry life. Just thinking about it made me feel like Alice falling into Wonderland.

"My house, too," I whispered, and crumpled the napkin into a ball I tossed from hand to hand, Mamma watching me all the time.

I looked up at the tall ceiling, painted a blue pretty as a springtime sky. Pictured myself sitting in one of the mahogany chairs in the dining room, maybe even one with arms at the head of the table, for my birthday or Confirmation. If this were my house, I could visit France and New York like they were handy as the grocery, that and play tennis at The Links, besides. Mr. Patrick would drive me all the way to the Ursuline School, where the girls wore white cotton gloves for assemblies, 'cause, "That's where I would have sent a daughter," Mrs. Castleberry told me once when she read my report card.

I dropped the napkin. It looked like the Sunday paper after Harper had gotten through with it.

"Sorry," I said to Mamma.

"Me, too," she said, and picked it up to smooth it.

"And if this were our house, you'd be able to keep the book Doctor Prout gave you on the sofa table, where the Castleberry Bible is now? Somebody'd be folding these towels for you, right?"

A breeze blew the sheers into the library. They billowed like sails.

Mamma scrunched her face and bit her bottom lip. I knew she was trying not to cry. I reached up and straightened her apron covered her chest. I thought of how Mamma and me worked in the Castleberry house most every day. We knew where everything belonged, took care of the fine china and the comfortable furniture, even Mrs. Castleberry herself as though they were our very own. We even had a set of keys, the keychain monogrammed with a large scrolled *C*. Everything in place, but not the way Mamma had wanted.

I leaned against Old Doctor Castleberry's desk.

"Mamma," I asked her, "did you love my Daddy at all?"

She looked at me like she was surprised and sad at the same time.

"Actually, Orla, I love him more and more the longer he's gone. He gave us his good name. And he took care of us, even knowing I always wanted something more. He understood St. Suplice's ways, or at least accepted them better than I do. He didn't bother about trying to make life different than it was. He was a good man, an honest man. He deserved more than a wife who wanted somebody else's life. I never had the chance to tell him that."

Mamma's face looked pinched, like her mouth hurt inside. I wished I could unremember the drawer.

She stood up and opened a new package of clothespins.

Tad's feet pounded up the back steps from the shed. He walked through the kitchen, stopping like he always did to look at the painting of the bull fight in the foyer.

"No, Ma'am, no eyeglasses out there," he said to Mamma.

He walked to each table in the room while I checked the desk drawer. Nothing in it but a telephone book and some maps of "Greater New Orleans." I looked next shelf by shelf all around the room. Mostly yellow-and-white *National Geographic* magazines, medical journals, and the Harvard Classics. One *Screen Life*.

"Ha," I surprised myself out loud, 'cause no doubt Mrs. Castleberry would have hollered at her husband, too.

Mamma has hundreds of movie magazines at home in the nightstand and in two piles side of her bed. I read most of them when we pick them up used from May at her Village Hair Shoppe every month where we get our hair trimmed. I love to study the makeup the actresses wear, specially the eye makeup. Nobody in St. Suplice wears as much eye makeup as Elizabeth Taylor or Natalie Wood. Heck, most of the ladies only put lipstick on for funerals and high school graduation.

Every night after we finish taking turns reading *Oliver Twist* or *David Copperfield* out loud, Mamma picks two

Screen Life copies to read after I go up to bed. She knows everything about movie stars.

"Hollywood," she says sometimes, when she soaks her feet after ironing for Mrs. Haldecott and working at Mrs. Castleberry's all day. "There's life, Orla, and then there's Hollywood."

When she paints her toes and fingernails and wears the scoop-necked turquoise dress Mrs. Haldecott's younger daughter tired of, Mamma looks like a movie star herself. All she needs for a cover shot on *Screen Life* is to fling back her long black hair and smile at Eddie Fisher or Richard Burton over her left shoulder.

Doesn't make sense for Mrs. Castleberry to yell at Mamma about the magazines. They're just something we read for fun 'cause we get them for free. Mamma's probably read more real books than people even went to college. Mrs. Castleberry should know that. Maybe she just gets embarrassed by some of the stories in them. She didn't want Mamma to marry her son, imagine what she thinks of Elizabeth Taylor stealing somebody else's husband. Mamma's right about Mrs. Castleberry. Sometimes she acts like she's God.

"Look, Mamma," I said, and handed her the copy.

She rolled it into a cylinder and thumped it like a club on Doctor Castleberry's desk. Then she let it roll open again, left it on the desk, and straightened the scarf she had tied around her head.

She unclamped her lips and asked, "You two finding anything interesting in here?"

"Look," I pointed to the villa.

"Is that the orphanage?" Mamma asked.

On the back of the picture, the writing said, "The Contessa's home before the war."

84

"Must be, then," Mamma said, as the phone rang.

She walked out into the foyer to get it.

Tad said, "Looks like somebody took the picture from high up across the way."

The villa was shaped like a square O with a yard in the middle. I could see lawn furniture, even nicer than the Haldecott's. There were umbrellas and chaise lounges and a fountain. A body could tell the water was running even though the picture was still. All around the yard were arches. Upstairs had regular windows, but bigger, five across the front.

"Good," said Tad. "The last four notebooks are labeled War Diaries."

He opened the first volume, where a red tab was sticking out.

"Look at this, Orla," he said, excited like it was Christmas, "Old Doctor Castleberry wrote practically his own book."

Tad began to read:

> "I tried to prepare myself for what I would see. Before we shipped out, I even read writings by soldiers who had fought in previous wars. But I know now that actual war is nothing like the stories people tell. The stench of death is everywhere. Mostly there is agony and long suffering. Ugliness and pain. And right next to it, like an insult to the wounded, the beauty of the Italian landscape and centuries of art and culture."

Only dead thing besides regular garbage I ever smelled up close was Lizzy's dog before Harper. The old girl disappeared one day and didn't come home even after Mrs. Crowther set food out on the front stoop for her. Hester was her name. Most one week after she left, a bad smell, worse than rotten eggs, seemed to be coming from the shed. Mr. Crowther emptied the whole thing out. There were rakes and ladders, a wheelbarrow, some tires belonged to a tractor, all over the yard. Couple of garden snakes and plenty of spiders rushin' out like they'd been dismissed from school. But the smell was still there.

"You stay back, now," Mr. Crowther said.

Then he walked to the back of the shed, where the hydrangeas had grown together. Lizzy and I waited.

"Lordy and I'll be damned," he muttered, then came back around the shed with his arm covering his nose and mouth. Took some deep breaths, real slow.

"No need for you to bother yourselves going back there. Poor Hester is surely dead."

Then he went in to tell Mrs. Crowther. Soon as he closed the screen door behind him, Lizzy and I ran to see. I knew right away we shouldn't have. Before we even had time to cover our faces, I felt dizzy and, quick as a firefly lighting, I threw up. Lizzy, too. It was the maggots did it as much as the smell. Where Hester's eyes used to be were two wriggling circles. Them and crawling bugs, flies, too. Something with teeth had bitten chunks out of Hester's stomach.

We ran back around and sat on the picnic table bench with our heads in our hands, spitting out the vomit much as we could. Lizzy cried.

Seems like every time I really want to see something or find something out, after I do I'm sorry I wanted to in the first place. I'll never think of Hester leaping up to catch a fly ball anymore. Only see her maggoty eyes. Or Mr. Cowles, before he took to beating his own children, the time he hugged Denny all wet after winning the breast-stroke.

Tad sat down with a thud in Old Doctor Castleberry's chair with wheels and continued reading:

> *"People who require nothing more than their crops and their families are starving. Today I saw a boy no older than my own son Prout offer himself to a soldier in exchange for some rations. A girl—"*

"Offer what himself?" I said.

I licked my fingers and tried to rub some paint off my arm. Tad didn't answer. He crossed his legs, first right on top of left, then left on top of right. Then he pulled at his lips and chin with his fingers. He cracked his knuckles twice.

"If you don't know, I'm not telling," he said.

He started counting the pages in the notebook, turning one page after another. Still didn't talk. I punched his shoulder. He pretended it didn't hurt, just kept counting.

"Then you don't know," I said, walked around the back of the chair, and punched him on the other side.

He dropped the book on the desk in front of him, spun around in the chair, and stood up.

"Knock it off, Orla, you're such a baby."

He pushed me out of his way and walked around the desk. I stuck out my tongue behind him, sat down in his place, and reached for the book, but he stretched across and grabbed it before I could look at it myself. I spun round and round like I didn't care.

"For sex," he said, finally. "He let the guy have sex with him for money or food."

My feet dragged the chair to a stop. My face was getting red, red and hot. I felt heavy as a sack of flour full. Tad knowin' about sex was different from him knowin' history. I looked up toward the highest shelves like I was searching for another book. I hoped Tad couldn't hear my heart pounding through my chest. I got up slow, felt like falling, and walked, watching one foot follow th'other, to the bookcase farthest away from him.

"Oh, yeah, that's what I thought," I said.

My voice was a brick falling.

Tad walked around and sat down in Dr. Castleberry's chair again. I turned to look. He just sat there with his hands folded top the desk, serious-like. Staring straight ahead.

I wondered how the boy and the soldier did it. Didn't know two men could do it. If men could, maybe women did, too. I closed my eyes. Felt dizzy, like after too much sun. Hot and cold at the same time. My privates felt squishy, tingly.

Old Doctor Castleberry's swivel chair squeaked as Tad leaned back. I looked at him. He started reading the notebook again. Held it over his head, pushed the chair back from the desk so his legs reached long in front of him. Looked like a human V.

Crotch. That was the word jumped into my head. Tad's crotch. I felt like steam.

He read on.

> "A girl about five years of age sitting in the middle of a piazza, lapping water out of the fountain, trying to clean her soiled body."

Soiled. That's what Mrs. Castleberry called Tad's Aunt Fern Mae. She and Mrs. Haldecott were having tea one day when I helped serve. Just when I picked up the sandwich tray, Mrs. Haldecott said, "Today is Fern Mae's birthday. She's thirty years old."

I remember Mrs. Castleberry taking her time folding her white lace tea napkin on her lap. She sighed a big sigh and said, "That poor child was soiled before she even had a chance."

Soiled. It didn't make sense. Fern Mae hadn't done anything bad. Some hooligan's fault she had a baby. If soiled had something to do with sex, was everybody had a baby soiled? Mamma? Mrs. Castleberry, too? Did Denny Cowles soil Alice Carroll when he wouldn't let her have one of the park swings till she let him look up her dress? He tried to make me do it, too. When I wouldn't, he grabbed my skirt. I spat right in his face.

"I'll tell Mamma!" I said.

He let go, but pushed me right on my chest. Touched my nipples.

"You don't have anything worth looking at anyhow," he said.

I pretended I didn't care. But I did. Felt dirty, too, like his sayin' what he wanted to do was just as bad as his doing it. Like it was my fault he wanted to.

Soiled.

Tad dropped the photo album onto the desk.

"Orla, this is great!" Tad said. "This is like being there."

He never looked up, just kept turning one page after another.

"I think it's disgusting," I said. "Kids all filthy, missin' body parts. Plus, we don't even know what those Italian words mean, let alone how to say them."

"Doesn't matter," Tad said. "I understand most of it."

He read aloud some more.

"After Rome, we drove north to Florence and retreated to a small town above the Arno River, called Fiesole. So old is this town that the Etruscans had built an amphitheater into the

hillside there. Villas abound, and the hills are filled with wheat and olive trees. At the top of the town is a monastery. When we arrived, hoping for some respite from operating, we discovered large numbers of children living in the courtyard, the nuns feeding them soup and offering them relative safety.

"Maybe we can find pictures of this place in another file," Tad said.

He stood up and went back to the shelves. It took what seemed like forever, long enough for me to count two hundred books one side of the room, but, finally, he discovered two photographs. One showed a boy with a bowl to his mouth, the other a nun handing out blankets to some children.

Tad started reading aloud to me again while I picked up a magnifying glass on Old Doctor Castleberry's desk so I could get a better look at the people's faces.

"This morning I made rounds at the small, makeshift hospital in Fiesole's hotel at the request of one of the nuns. There I met Contessa Beatrice D'Annunzio, who was sitting by the bedside of her eight-year-old son, Paolo. His left leg had been blown off in the grenade explosion in Florence that had killed his father. He had lost so much blood that he was already unconscious."

"Stop it, Tad."

He looked up at me like I was nuts.

"What do you expect, Orla? It's a war. Go hide upstairs with your mother if you can't take it."

"Jerk," I said.

90

"Jerk, yourself," Tad muttered.

I sat down on the polished wood floor.

"Keep going," I said.

He went on.

> "The Contessa told me that the authorities were calling it an accident. But her husband had been unwilling to ally himself with the Fascisti.
>
> She kept stroking her son's face. Paolo's eyes were closed. Her fingers were long and slender, like those of a pianist. We spoke in whispers. When she asked me how long, I told her not very. That's when she called me "un uomo onesto"—an honest man. She asked me to return later. I told her I would.
>
> When I did, late in the afternoon, she was alone, sitting in the dark by the empty bed. She looked like a statue, a Madonna. I'll never forget what she said. It haunted me.
>
> 'Dottore, all I have now is money.'"

I stood up.

"I'm going outside."

Tad didn't look up.

"Suit yourself," he said, and turned the page.

Later, after Mamma was asleep, I got the emergency flashlight out the junk drawer in the kitchen. It gave enough light so I could draw a boy trying to hop on one leg. He kept falling down in my sketches. When I finally went to bed, I left him sitting down crying. A frog leaping onto the sleeping porch screen 'bout scared me to death. I could see the muscles in his legs quivering.

Chapter Fourteen

Somewhere in the attic, Mrs. Castleberry had an old easel. Next morning, before we had even arrived, she had Mr. Patrick, her handyman, bring it on down to the garden. Time Mamma and Tad and I got there, Mr. Patrick had washed it all down so's it was ready for me. I put on my straw hat and sat under a big green umbrella Mr. Patrick set up "so you won't have to squint," he told me.

Mr. Patrick was the oldest man in town. He told me he was born "when Queen Victoria of England was conquering all kinds of places on earth, showed no signs of dying, and television hadn't been thought of yet." He used to have a wife cooked for Mrs. Castleberry. But she died before I was old enough to recall her.

While I was fixin' up my paper on the easel, he said, "Mrs. Castleberry's exciting herself silly over this visit come August. Even got us listening to Italian music, opera."

Sure enough, before I so much as opened the paints, I heard music coming out the upstairs windows. I didn't understand the words, but the voices sounded like they were singin' big feelings. Like when a body watches a parade, or if I get an A+ on a composition. The words were drawn out long and full, like clouds gone slate-colored, heavy with rain, or a cow's ink-deep eyes.

"I think Mrs. Castleberry's planning a big party when these Italians come," Mr. Patrick said. "That's what she told me. Well, Orla, you get on to your work, I'll go tend to the roses."

At least out here, I thought, I won't have to think about anybody dying.

From where I was sitting, looking at the Castleberry house with the sun at my back, I felt like I was on an island. Inside the picket fence all kinds of bushes and flowers grew tall so's a body really couldn't see into the yard from the street.

For Mamma, it was a work island—big laundry Monday, delicates Friday, silver-polishing and general cleaning in-between. Only time Mamma got to be company was Easter morning. Then she looked nice as Mrs. Castleberry, Miss Foster, even. Wore flower colors—pink and violet, yellow, sometimes. Picture hat big as a moon. White gloves with pearl buttons. High heels and stockings felt like silk.

I heard flapping above the opera voices. Mamma hung over the porch rail outside Mrs. Castleberry's dressing room beating a rug. She looked small, her face hovering over the rug unfurled like a blue and gold banner. Her features gauzy from the glare of the sun. A white triangle scarf covered her hair. A blue-and-white ticking apron, like the nuns wore who cleaned St. Marguerite's, hid her shape. Her white sneakers peeked from between the rails. She slid in and out the French doors like a spirit, shaking ivory bedclothes into the air in great, billowing bursts. My mother, Minerva, the Castleberry house ghost.

"Mamma," I waved.

She lifted her head, looked down to me, and my brush started moving like it was alive on its own.

I mixed the colors to show her shades—fog, paste, dough not risen. Almost invisible. Mamma had no clothes of her own.

My brush flew. Tall and long, her legs, her arms. Hands busy, fingers moving, wouldn't be still until Sunday when she'd turn into herself, take off her apron and scarf, put rouge on her cheeks, and rest.

I looked up from the easel. Mamma had vanished. I kept painting till lunchtime.

"That Minerva?"

Mr. Patrick came up behind me. I turned with my fingers to my lips.

"Shh. I want to surprise her."

He wiped his forehead with the red bandanna he always had stickin' out his back pocket.

"Too pale. You should make her brighter. Did you take a look at the veranda? Varnished the floor last week. Put a nice gloss on it. That nigger minister was the first to walk on it just dried. Mrs. Castleberry had him and his missus to tea. They were busy writing, all three of them, into notebooks, planning something important, it seemed to me. "

He blew his nose real loud.

"She shouldn't be involving herself with them. I don't like it, not one bit. Not that she's asked my opinion."

Mr. Patrick brushed some leaves out his hair.

If somebody nice as Mr. Patrick didn't like the reverend, maybe there was something not to like.

"Strange how she treats them better than some of us White," he said, raking the weeds into a pile.

It's true, I guess. Long as I've known him, I've never seen Mr. Patrick sit down at one of Mrs. Castleberry's tables. When she offers him food or iced tea, she leaves it outside on the veranda, sometimes not even on a plate, but top a paper napkin unfolded, and the tea in a paper cup. He's too old to be making sure the walk's edges are straight. Down on his knees, his groans sounding like the cows lowing in the way-off field. Uses a clipper, then picks up the leavings and crawls ahead a few feet to clip again. Has to grab onto one of the chaise lounges just to stand up.

Just before she went upstairs with Mamma earlier, Mrs. Castleberry told him she was glad he had gotten his eye glass prescription changed.

"I know you'll have no trouble spotting the weeds now," she said.

Why was she friends with the reverend? Never saw her with any other Negroes. Maybe she was getting old enough to be confused.

Mamma came downstairs and outside. She hurried over to us.

"The radio just announced that Mr. Cowles lost his job," Mamma said, "for the damages he caused over to St. Marguerite's."

Mr. Patrick stretched his back.

"He shouldn't have done what he did," Mamma said. "It's a wonder he didn't think. Why, Bridget will have to bake double while he cools his heels not getting his weekly pay. He's lost two good jobs, she told me, driving some financiers around bayou country. Kathleen hasn't let go her mother's hand one minute since the trouble. And Denny's so angry he's taken to kicking the dog. No black body every did Jimmy Cowles wrong I know of."

Mr. Patrick coughed.

"A man does something hot-headed, it's almost always his family that suffers. Either of you two want some water?"

He went toward the kitchen.

"Come on," Mamma said, "let me get some for you."

I stayed behind to get back to Mamma's portrait. Nobody bothered me the rest of the afternoon. Every now and then I heard Tad reading aloud to himself in the library. Sounded just like the evening news. Kept wondering what interested Mrs. Castleberry about the reverend, how she let his wife sit down in the company chairs while making Mamma work like a nigger herself.

Dusk was starting by the time I carried Mamma's portrait into the shed and hid it aside the rake closet. Mamma came out the kitchen with a shopping bag of leftovers from Mrs. Castleberry for our supper. Smelled like chicken, roasted potatoes, and onions.

"I'll carry it," I said.

Mamma handed me the bag with Bergdorf Goodman, New York City, on one side. She took off her scarf and shook her hair loose.

"You coming?" I hollered in to Tad.

I heard Old Doctor Castleberry's chair roll across the floor.

"Not yet," he said. "Want to read one more file. I'll be by after breakfast tomorrow."

"Suit yourself," I answered.

I took a look at Mr. Patrick's floor. Never noticed before how many seats there were. All wicker or wood-slatted. Four rocking chairs, two chaise lounges, two gliders, and six club chairs. And tables, for card-playing and eating. Only thing was, I never saw a body on them 'cepting during the Easter Egg Hunt.

Mamma and I made our way out of the yard. I turned back toward the big screen door.

"Night, Mrs. Castleberry."

"Bonne nuit, Orla," I heard from the phone table in the foyer.

It was still hot as an oven. Mamma and I walked real slow.

"Mamma, why doesn't Mrs. Castleberry have company?"

Mamma wiped her face with her scarf. She cleared her throat.

"There was a time, Orla, when the Castleberry place was busy most every day. Many a time, Mrs. Castleberry asked Mrs. Haldecott if she could spare my mother and father to help Mr. Patrick and his late wife over here. Old Doctor Castleberry used to invite all kinds of folks down here, especially from Nashville, where he lectured every month."

Mamma stopped to tie up her hair.

"Why'd they stop coming?" I asked.

Mamma blew a ladybug off her arm.

"I think Old Doctor Castleberry's death hit Mrs. Castleberry quite hard. She didn't like people feeling sorry for her, so she'd cut off their sympathies by snapping at them. She got the reputation of being too uppity for her own good. Wouldn't accept the usual condolences and offers of food or supper invitations. She even stopped going to the country club Friday nights. Lord knows, she barked at me plenty every week I helped her with the laundry and in the pantry."

I kicked a clump of dirt out in front of me like it was a ball.

"Did you get angry?"

Mamma laughed.

"Of course."

Then she whistled under her breath. Not a tune, really, more like a bayou hawk calling.

"Well?" I said.

"One day, almost suppertime..."

She sounded like she was reading me a story when I was little.

"... I dropped one of her glass candlesticks still slippery from the sink. It crashed to the floor into dozens of tiny pieces just as she walked in."

I thought of Mrs. Castleberry's crystal lined up in the corner cabinet. Each piece next to another that matched. One set trimmed with gold, another with silver, "these for champagne, those for red wine, dear."

"What happened?" I asked.

Mamma whistled again.

"I got a broom and dust pan from the utility closet and was brushing the mess into the garbage pail when Mrs. Castleberry grabbed me by the shoulders and shook me hard. 'Minerva,' she said, 'you are the clumsiest person I know.'"

I couldn't imagine Mrs. Castleberry doing something like that to me. Even though I help out, I never have to get really dirty or do anything difficult. Mostly I'm there to learn "how to be a lady."

"That's what I want you to be," Mrs. Castleberry told me when I was just five. Mamma had gone upstairs to iron when she said it. "I'll teach you how to be a lady."

For me, Mrs. Castleberry's island is like a special school, for learning music, or manners, like the country club girls go to after regular classes. Mrs. Castleberry's not exactly a teacher, more like a bossy governess, the kind in some fairy tales.

"Come now," she'll say, "we'll learn how to set the table for high tea."

Most she ever touches me is to pat my shoulder when she reads my report card or when I pronounce a French word correctly. Once she blew me a kiss before she went to France for a month.

"What did you do?"

Mamma stopped walking, put her hands on her hips, turned and looked right into my eyes.

"I stood up tall, pushed her hands off me, looked right back at her, and said, 'And you, Mrs. Castleberry, are a bitch!'"

"Really?" I said. "What did she do?"

Mamma looked into my eyes again.

"She cried."

Mamma said it like it was an announcement, like she was on a stage.

"She did?"

I tried to imagine Mrs. Castleberry crying. I thought I saw her eyes mist over a little when she heard Mrs. Haldecott's daughter had a baby stillborn, but I couldn't be sure. She had started saying her rosary right away, and she always carried a lace handkerchief anyway.

I looked at Mamma strange. She sounded proud as Lizzy after she had dunked the winning basket against St. Felice's.

"Yes, she sat down at the kitchen table and cried."

Mamma was smiling, looking right through me, smiling and smiling.

"Did you feel bad? Did you apologize?"

Mamma started walking again, faster. I hopped a few steps to catch up. She whistled some more.

"For what?" she said.

"For calling her a bitch, Mamma."

Mamma straightened her shoulders and walked like Miss Yvette in her high heels, like she had to catch a train to New York.

"I certainly did not," she said.

Her voice sounded sure as the fire horn at noon. She turned to me again, looked at me like I'd asked her something silly.

"Why ever would I, Orla. Why ever would I even think to."

The way she said it didn't sound like a question.

"Because it's mean, Mamma! I can't believe you. You'd be furious if I talked like that."

She wasn't even listening. I watched her walk ahead of me. She rounded the bend.

"Stop," I said. "Mamma, stop."

Mamma stood and turned around.

"I've told you before, Orla, Mrs. Castleberry is different with me than with you. To her, I'm no more than a laundress, someone to clean up her messes. But you, you're...."

She stopped talking. She drew herself up, crossed her arms over her chest, breathed in like she was sucking the air right out of the day, and waited, waited long before she exhaled.

"What?" I said. "What am I, Mamma?"

I felt all alone. I ran, caught up to her, pulled at both her arms. She wrapped them around me and squeezed me tight.

"You are the future," she said.

She sounded as serious as Walter Cronkite looking right out the television screen. Held me so tight I had to stare right up into her face.

"You are the only future Mrs. Castleberry's got."

Mamma sounded sure, angry-sure, the way she did that time she told me to march myself right back to the school gymnasium and tell Mrs. Ruck, that I "certainly would be coming to the Father/Daughter Dance with Mr. Patrick, old as he is and nice as my own Grandpa McKay was." And "you just stand up straight, Orla, and don't worry one bit about her being a so-called grown-up. You tell her, you tell her clearly in front of all the other Girl Scout mothers who don't have to work, who think they rule the world, that you'll be there, ready to dance with Mr. Patrick."

I did. I did go back and tell Mrs. Ruck. But only that I'd be there with Mr. Patrick. She gave a little sniff and rolled her eyes over to Mrs. Marquand, then made a check mark with her pencil looked just sharpened in the "yes" column of her response list.

Mrs. Castleberry must have thought Mamma was at least partly right. She didn't fire her. Still lent her books. One time, when Mamma had the flu last December, she even had Mr. Patrick drive her over to our house with broth, chicken broth she had made herself, she told me, "like my petite mère made me when I felt poorly, too."

In her bed, Mamma had sipped the soup right from the bowl while Mrs. Castleberry watched from the doorway. I sat on the edge of the bed between the two of them waiting for something to happen. Even though nothing did, I felt the same as I do whenever I overhear Miss Foster tell the janitor there's going to be a fire drill. Nervous, ready to jump up and get out, like there were real flames.

Chapter Fifteen

On the screened-in part of our own veranda later that night, by the light from a reading lamp I borrowed from the library room, I started painting one of the Castleberry rocking chairs from memory. Then I went in and found the yearbook from Mamma and Prout's high school graduating class. I studied Prout's face. It was long, and his nose looked like his mamma's. His hair was parted on the side, with a wave over his forehead. He was smiling, but with his mouth closed. Before long, I found myself painting him into his chair. Only in my picture he wasn't smiling, he was thinking about his daddy.

One time, when Mamma had gone to the grocery for her, Mrs. Castleberry and I sat at the same table on the veranda she told me Prout and Old Doctor Castleberry used every night the doctor was home. The two of them played chess.

"My husband thought it trained the mind," Mrs. Castleberry said.

"Tad is teaching me," I told her. "He made a board out of some cardboard Mr. Carroll didn't need, and pieces from clay. We painted them, even the rooks."

At that, she stood up and said, "Well, then, I'll have to find Prout's old set so you and Tad can become as expert as they were."

She never did. Or maybe she just forgot. I got to thinking how Prout might have it himself up in Boston. How his face might have looked while he waited for his daddy to make the next move.

"Orla," Mamma called from inside, "time for bed."

She walked onto the porch in my Daddy's hospital robe.

"Aren't you sleepy? What are you painting?" she asked.

I was trying to get Prout's mouth right. It was a problem. I wanted to miss my own Daddy, but hadn't known him long enough, the way Prout did his. I wanted to paint Prout's mouth to say, "Dad?" then realize his daddy couldn't answer.

"Why, that's Prout Castleberry," Mamma said.

She stared at him, then me, then him again. Touched the top of my head. I stood up and threw my arms around her.

"Don't leave me," I said.

Mamma held me tight.

"What ever gave you such an idea?" she said.

I held on and on.

Finally I asked, "Mamma, do you think Mrs. Castleberry'll let me borrow one of her opera records and a record player?"

"Let's just ask her," Mamma said.

She crossed her arms over her chest so her hands reached her shoulders, like when she had seen my Daddy's pajamas.

"Mamma," I said.

But she didn't seem to hear me. Her eyes were closed.

"Mamma?"

She didn't answer, just rubbed her left arm up and down with her right for a long time. I watched the upstairs lights blink off at the Carroll house across the street. Then, like she woke up after a dream, she said, "You go ahead and paint until you're done, if you want to. I'm going to bed. Remember to shut the door."

I heard her go into her bedroom. I put down my paintbrush and picked up the yearbook again. I traced the outline of Prout's face with my finger. Looked into his eyes. Some flying creature buzzed across my forehead. I brushed it away and felt my hair. My fingers combed my curls again and again. My heart began to drum. I stood up, walked to the window nearest the lamplight, stared into the glass. Myself, the same as always, I decided. Drum, drum, drum. The humid air slithered across the windowpanes like wavy electric eels. My face trembled like it would have in water. I stared at my forehead. Ran my hands through my curls again. Bowed my head to the floor, then shook it hard. Jerked it back up and looked again. Still the waves fell back into place onto my forehead as natural as night, looked back at me curved and glowing, alive somehow in the window, new though not different, familiar still, the way things get when light shifts and, suddenly, shadows disappear.

Chapter Sixteen

The day before Fourth of July, I was all set to paint the cement bird bath outside her dining room when Mrs. Castleberry waved out her bedroom window. Her white handkerchief fluttered up and down like a dove in a magician's hat. She strained her voice above Mr. Patrick's mowing.

"Orla, dear, I want to show you the *figuristi*."

I stood and moved closer under the window, looked up and listened hard.

"The what?"

But she'd already tucked herself back inside. I walked back to the easel to put my brush down.

"Here I come," I yelled up to the screen.

Upstairs, linens were lying all over the beds. In the guest room, tablecloths and napkins with the letter C embroidered in violet to match Mrs. Castleberry's china. In Doctor Prout's old room, sheets and pillowcases trimmed with the delicate lace she made Mamma starch. Mamma was sorting each by size on Doctor Prout's bed, some standard, some larger, a few smaller ones. The steam iron hissed and the smell of bleach reminded me of the nurse's room at school.

Mrs. Castleberry stood waiting for me at the top of the stairs dressed like she was going to the club for lunch, then led me into her bedroom and on past the louvered doors into her dressing room. I'd never been there before. Mamma always made me wait outside by the bureau with the statue of St. Therese of Lisieux on top. When I was little I wanted her to talk to me so I could have my own miracle and be listed in Grammie's prayer book.

"Now then," Mrs. Castleberry said.

I followed behind her. The dressing room ceiling was so high I had to pull my head all the way back to see the whirring fan in the middle. The air it whooshed around us was warm. The morning light came bright through the French doors that led out onto a small balcony where Mrs. Castleberry sometimes napped on her chaise lounge in the afternoon. The lace that covered the door panes looked like wedding cake frosting. There was a big closet separate from the wall, "an armoire, dear," she told me, some ordinary bureaus, and a dressing table with a lavender skirt, but no ruffles. Shelves painted lavender, too, only lighter, were stacked one on top of the other all over the room, high up, even around and over the French doors. Each one was filled with plaster figures—cats and birds, roses, too.

"Orla," she said, "I thought you'd enjoy these."

Mrs. Castleberry handed me a rose the color of lemon meringue with little gold sparkles on the petals. I held it with two hands.

"What are they?" I asked.

She put her hand on my shoulder, patted it twice, then took the rose from me and set it on her dressing table. Its petals looked real enough to smell. Then she sat down on her dressing table stool. You could hardly tell it had wheels. She held her knees together so still that her legs made straight lines. Her stockings fit like a second skin. Even the buckles on her navy blue shoes touched, exactly side by side.

"They are gesso figurines, plaster figures to which gold leaf and other paints can adhere. The larger ones, these statues..."

She stood up, reached over my head to a higher shelf, and pointed to a donkey pulling a cart of hay. Each piece of plaster straw was at least three shades of yellows and browns.

"...these statues were all made by the children at La Casa dei Bambini to help support the orphanage."

I studied all the pieces around me. The animals could have filled a miniature barnyard.

"How long did it take them to make all these?" I asked.

Mrs. Castleberry smiled. The statues were grouped by type—a flock of geese, wreaths of vines, lambs, oranges, lemons, and limes.

She went back to her stool. This time she pushed the stool closer to the dressing table with her feet, crossed her legs, and leaned back on her elbows. Her legs looked younger than the rest of her, like they could keep up kicking with me in a swimming race.

"They were made over a period of years. When my husband was still alive," she sat up straighter, "the Contessa wrote us that she wanted to find a way to teach the children to make a living when they became old enough to leave the orphanage."

Mrs. Castleberry motioned for me to sit on the floor. I felt like I was in school.

Mr. Patrick's mower growled under the French doors.

She continued.

"So she contacted the authorities in Lucca, a city known for its *figuristi*—artisans of such pieces—and asked if they would find her some craftspeople who would be willing to move to Fiesole and teach the orphans."

I thought of the one-armed boy and the dirty girl in the pictures Tad had found painting the animals. What if they didn't want to? Maybe they'd rather have been farmers or chefs. I stood up and walked from shelf to shelf.

Mrs. Castleberry kept quiet for a while and watched me move from the fruits to the geese, the roses to the baskets of wheat.

"Egidio Ferraro, his wife Emilia, and son Eduardo agreed to the move. Still today, and Egidio must be at least eighty years old, I imagine, they operate a workshop at the orphanage. My husband used to send a catalog of their handiwork to everyone on our Christmas card list every year."

I thought of how it would be running through a field of real wheat tall as me. Leaping off a barn loft into hay that was soft and scratchy. Milking a cow myself.

"Most of our acquaintances made at least one purchase a year to lend support to the orphanage."

Mrs. Castleberry laughed out loud. I could see her teeth.

"We made them feel obligated."

I turned from her again and stopped before an angel who sparkled silver with gold wings. Her lips were open in the shape of a big O.

"My favorite pieces, though, are not here, Orla. Come."

Mrs. Castleberry stood up from her stool, smoothed her skirt, and shook her left arm the way a body does when it's been in the same position too long and tingles. She put out her other hand, so I took it while she led me to the attic door. We passed Mamma, who was spraying starch on the lace and listening to the eleven o'clock radio show that played old Broadway show tunes. Singers were spelling *"O-K-L-A-H-O-M-A"* very loudly. Mrs. Castleberry looked in and nodded.

The door stuck, "It never fails to, my dear," she said, and I had to help her pull it hard to open.

When it did, sunshine streamed down the stairway like in holy pictures. Mrs. Castleberry's heels sounded heavy on the wooden stairs, and she walked slower than usual. She held the walls each side of her like she was trying to keep them from crushing her in between. As I followed behind, the sun covered me from head to toe like a hooded robe. At the top of the stairs, the light was so strong, I had to blink. Tiny floating dust puffs glimmered all around me. Tinker Bell, I thought.

Mrs. Castleberry looked almost tall. Most of the attic held the larger gesso pieces that filled or surrounded the crèche Mr. Patrick set up on the veranda every Christmas. She stood right over the wooden and straw stable. It reached her neck.

"Every piece here was a gift from the Contessa," she said.

She waved her arm around the attic, cutting through the glittering air like she held a wand. My cheeks tingled with warmth. Then Mrs. Castleberry looked annoyed for a moment, shook her arm again, and rubbed both hands around her neck. On the floor next to her right foot Baby Jesus lay in an orange crate stuffed with tissue paper.

"I remember the first time I saw Him," I said.

I was four years old, and Mamma told me Mrs. Castleberry had said to bring me with her to prepare Christmas morning brunch. I was dressed in a green velvet dress Mamma had pieced together from Mrs. Haldecott's remnants. As we walked into the Castleberry yard, I saw lights twinkling on the veranda.

I let go Mamma's hand and ran toward them. My shiny black shoes sounded pat, pat, pat on the ground. I tripped on the steps. The greens on the veranda smelled like the long-needle pine same size as me Mamma and I had decorated the night before with red ribbons and gingerbread cookies.

"Baby Jesus, Baby Jesus!" I'd yelled, and made for the crib.

"No!" Mamma said, and pulled me away, but just then Mrs. Castleberry came outside in a shiny silver robe and slippers with sparkly stones on them. She smelled like peppermint and looked just like the angels kneeling either side of Jesus. She picked up the Baby, sat down on the veranda steps, patted a spot next to her for me to sit down, too, then put Him in my arms.

"Rock the Baby," she told me. "Rock Him like this."

The two of us sat there rocking Baby Jesus. Mamma went inside. Mrs. Castleberry sang in French, one verse then another. Pretty soon, I was singing, too, singing "*le divin enfant*," laughing with Mrs. Castleberry.

Even now, Jesus' lips were full, a bubble of red.

Mrs. Castleberry squinted at me from over her silver half-glasses. She stretched her arms out in front of her, clenched and unclenched her fists if like she was tired from holding something heavy.

"Yes. And every year a new piece arrives mid-November. The Contessa is quite methodical."

I touched the top of Mary's head. Her halo burned gold.

"Are they heavy?" I asked.

Mrs. Castleberry lifted Mary up like she were made of cotton candy, then put her down in slow motion. She arched her neck from side to side.

"Not at all, but easily breakable. Mr. Patrick tells me he worries every year he starts down the stairs."

Maybe he'd let Tad and me help him this time. Baby Jesus was the same size as a real baby, but the oxen were bigger than Lizzy's dead dog.

"I really like that angel," I said. "The way his eyes look right at me."

Mrs. Castleberry walked over to the one with Gabriel painted in scrolled gold letters below his feet. She wobbled a little and caught the crèche with her hand.

"That's the gold leaf I mentioned earlier," she said, pointing to the letters. She rubbed her left arm like her muscles hurt. Rolled her head in a circle.

"This Angel Gabriel was the first piece to arrive. I'll not forget the day the postman rang the doorbell and lowered a large crate onto the floor ever so carefully. When Prout and I opened it after he came home from school, real straw fell out in sheaves from around the statue, so we had a ready made floor for our manger."

Her voice got slower and softer as she spoke, so "carefully" and "manger" had big spaces of silence between each syllable. Then Mrs. Castleberry took off her glasses and rubbed her eyes.

"My," she said in a whisper, stretching her left arm out again, "I need some water. Quick-ly, Or-la. Wa-ter."

I gave her my hand to walk down the stairs with me, but she shook her head no, once to the left, once to the right, slow as a funeral march. She held onto the creche. Her face looked like it was crumbling. Her chin touched the top of her chest. Her lower lip drooped down.

"Mamma," I called, jumping down the steps two at a time. "Mamma!"

She wasn't ironing. Downstairs.

"Mamma," I yelled over the railing down into the front foyer.

111

"I'm coming, I'm coming," she said.

She stopped to tie her sneakers.

"Mrs. Castleberry's sick. She's..."

Crash.

Thud on wood, like from a height.

Mamma ran upstairs, yanked the attic door open and rushed up. I got to the bathroom, filled the sink cup, and followed behind. Mrs. Castleberry was stretched out on her side whimpering, Gabriel lay beside her, his feet cracked, his name shattered into jagged alphabet blocks, a G, a B, an E scattered like toys on the floor. Mrs. Castleberry's face was the color of ash, and every time she took a breath, it hurt. She scrunched her eyes closed.

"Here's your water, Mrs. Castleberry," I said, and Mamma lifted her head off the floor.

She tried to drink, but her breath came again and she gasped instead. Mamma took off her apron, rolled it into a long pillow, and put it under Mrs. Castleberry's neck.

"Stay here," she said. "I'm going to call the sheriff. We've got to get her to the hospital."

Mrs. Castleberry didn't even argue. She lay there, her eyes closed tight, clenching her teeth every time her chest moved. I grabbed her hands. She didn't grab back, just quivered on the floor, letting me hold on. My heart near burst out my chest. Mary, her hands outstretched with lifted palms, didn't make a move. Jesus lay in his cradle-crate, plump baby legs resting on the tissue paper. And Gabriel, broken now, too, kept his eyes on Mrs. Castleberry and me.

A miracle, I prayed. A miracle will happen now.

But nothing did. Sun beat the air around us, Mr. Patrick mowed the grass outside, and I couldn't tell if the buzzing in my ear was something Mrs. Castleberry heard, too.

Chapter Seventeen

Mamma came back with towels and a cold compress for Mrs. Castleberry's forehead.

She knelt alongside her and whispered into her ear, "Sheriff will be right here. You hold on now. We'll get you down to Convent right away."

Mrs. Castleberry gave no sign of hearing. Her breathing was short, little gasps at a time.

Shaking, I ran outside to Mr. Patrick, pulled at his shirt sleeve before he heard me and stopped mowing.

"Lord, Lord," he said, and started for the shed to wash his hands so he could come and help us.

I waited top of the veranda steps and counted. Five times to one hundred before I heard the siren.

Sheriff squealed into the driveway, then drove his car right over the front lawn to the steps. He ran in before me. Put his ear to Mrs. Castleberry's chest. Then he and Mamma lifted her like she was a rag doll, Sheriff had her arms, Mamma her legs.

"Now hold that door open far as it'll go, Orla," he said, and he and Mamma brought Mrs. Castleberry down the two flights of stairs, out the front door, down the veranda steps, and laid her on the back seat of the police car.

Mr. Patrick had a blanket in his hands and made the sign of the cross when he saw her.

"Best call Prout, Minerva," he said. "You know where she keeps the numbers."

Mamma nodded and Mrs. Castleberry groaned and tried to raise herself up from the seat.

"Easy, now," the sheriff told her. "No need to move, I'm going to get you right to the hospital."

He covered her with a blanket. Her hands poked up and down, up and down, under it, the way water boils in a pan. She opened her mouth, closed it, opened it again. The poking got faster. Scratchy sounds came from her throat. Mamma leaned into the car window to hear. From the other side Mr. Patrick and I did the same.

"Or-la," she moaned.

I shuddered. My name sounded like gravel.

"Right here, Mrs. Castleberry. I'm right here."

I tried to sound normal, like Miss Foster tells us to do when there's an emergency, but my legs were shaking. Mrs. Castleberry turned her head to the side. Opened her eyes just for a moment. Tears streamed out of them into the lines in her face. I patted her legs under the blanket, then lifted the blanket to smooth the stockings made folds at her ankles now. Her feet fell limp, the right foot one way, the left one the other. They looked so sad and so old, I started crying, too.

Mamma opened the door, rolled up the window but for a crack, tucked the blanket under Mrs. Castleberry's shoulders and closed the door so's not to bump her head. Mr. Patrick

114

put his hands on my shoulders and moved me away from the car. Then he did the same as Mamma, watching out for Mrs. Castleberry's feet. The sheriff turned on the flashing lights, backed out of the yard, and sped away. Time we three walked up into the kitchen, we could hear the siren fading. House felt like a cave. Why had she said my name?

"Is she dying?" I asked.

We sat at the table where Mrs. Castleberry always wrote out the grocery list. Only her seat was empty.

"Don't know," Mamma said, and shrugged her shoulders.

Then she reached across the table and took both my hands in hers. After a while, she got up and stood over me, playing with my hair like she did when I was little. Mr. Patrick went to the miscellany drawer by the icebox and took out a pack of cigarettes. He lit one with a match from top of the stove, and blew a line of smoke out his mouth like the kind a plane makes across the sky. Mamma smoothed the wavy strands that wanted to go their own way, then shook my ponytail of curls like she would a just-dried bath towel. She rubbed my shoulders till they relaxed. But then I thought of Mrs. Castleberry dying again.

"Why don't you take care of closing up the attic, Orla," Mamma said, "while I let Father Carriere know. No sense calling Prout until we know what to tell him."

Mr. Patrick stood up. He tugged at his shirt. I could see white skin under where the collar usually covered his neck.

"I might as well go on with the yard work," he said. "I can't be of any use in here."

He shuffled back outside, mumbling "the good Lord" as he let the screen door slam.

I went back upstairs and unjammed the attic door while Mamma told Miss Colette, the church housekeeper, "Yes, it's an emergency."

115

There was a small hand broom and a dust pan in a box marked Cleaning/Christmas right near the crèche, so I brushed the broken statue pieces into a little pile. I wanted to see how many we could glue together. Maybe Gabriel could be saved.

I couldn't stand him upright now that he was crooked underneath, so I leaned him against the crèche. An envelope looked like parchment slid onto the floor from beneath his jagged robes. On the front, Prout Castleberry was written in faded black ink, looked like from a fountain pen. The envelope wasn't sealed. The glue seemed worn off. A piece of writing paper stuck out. I pulled it all the way. It was bordered with lilies and vines, Italian writing, a date, and names—*15 Agosto 1944, nata in Fiesole, Italia, Gabriella Castello, figlia di Beatrice D'Annunzio et il dottore Peter Clemson Castleberry,*

"Mamma," I called downstairs. "I found something of Old Doctor Castleberry's, I think."

Mamma met me on the second floor. I gave her the paper. She sat down on the settee and read the words aloud, a syllable at a time. Her eyes opened wide. She got up, went into the bathroom, opened the faucets and threw water on her face. She came back, read the letter a second time, this time to herself, and sat down on the settee again.

"What?" I asked her.

She seemed dazed, like she was surprised. She looked at me like I had just appeared.

"What does it say?"

Mamma stood up.

"It says," she told me, then again, "it says that Prout Castleberry is not an only child. He has an Italian sister."

I took the letter from her hands and looked at it again.

"How can she be Italian?" I asked. "Mrs. Castleberry's not...."

I caught my breath, sat down on the settee myself. Maybe she saw it, maybe Mrs. Castleberry saw the letter and that's why she screamed. Maybe she tried to put it back, to hide it again in the statue. Maybe he killed her, it's her husband's fault she's going to die.

"Why does everybody have secrets?" I yelled. "Secrets that other people find."

"Whatever has gotten into you?" Mamma said, and tried to hold me.

But I wouldn't let her.

"Let go," I struggled out of her arms. "Let me go."

I flew down the stairs and outside just as the phone rang. Threw myself across the veranda steps.

"Yes, I surely will. I'll call him right away," Mamma said.

I got up off the steps and tip-toed to the side of the screen door.

I listened as Mamma dialed.

"Yes, Doctor Prout Castleberry... family emergency... his mother is in intensive care, in Louisiana."

I leaned against the siding where she couldn't see me and listened hard.

Mamma tapped the pencil on the desk. Tap, tap, stop. Tap, tap, stop. Mr. Patrick turned off the lawn mower back of the house. A garbage truck drove by. Tap, tap...

"Prout."

Her voice caught like a mouse in a trap.

Then again, louder, "Prout."

I knew from how she said his name she was a cup overflowing, she was about to cry.

"Yes, Minerva."

Her voice got higher, like a crow's, circling, calling into an open space of sky.

She tapped the pencil the whole time, faster and faster till it fell out of her hand. It rolled till it caught the carpet by the front door.

"Your mother. Heart attack. Yes. Yes. The sheriff is there. No, don't know which doctor. Convent. Come. Prout, you must come."

Mamma was sobbing. I leaned as close to the screen door as I could to see. She held the phone with both her hands, lay the receiver down slowly, gently, like she was putting a baby to bed.

Chapter Eighteen

I didn't go into the attic again. Didn't want to see the statues now. Mamma and me didn't hardly talk, either. She just kept ironing and I folded till all the linens were ready for the Italians, whether they'd be coming or not. Then we put sheets on Prout's bed so it'd be ready for him when he got home.

Mr. Patrick drove us home just before dark. The scapular he usually hung from his rear view mirror was around his neck. Earlier he told Mamma he'd sleep in the maid's room at the Castleberry place in case anybody called or needed something done, so she'd hardboiled some eggs for him and washed some grapes.

"We'll see you right after the sun comes up," she said. "We'll walk up as usual."

Our little house looked the same as when we left it in the morning.

Mamma went into her room to change while I filled the tub with water hot as I could stand. I closed the bathroom door and watched the air turn to steam. Easing my way into the bath, I leaned my head back and felt the water lapping, my arms and legs like willow branches yielding.

Just when I was drifting easy as a raft, something familiar sounded from outside the bathroom door. Something I'd heard before. It wasn't Mamma's voice or the radio. It was music, Italian opera.

I stood up in the tub, let the water fall off me, stepped onto the rug that felt soft as cotton balls. I wrapped myself in a towel, shook the damp off my hair. Wiping steam off the mirror over the sink with my hands, I bowed to my reflection. Two voices were singing together. A man and a woman. One voice gliding into the other. Smooth as the skin on my arms.

I hung the towel to dry over the edge of the tub and pulled my nightgown over my head.

"Night, Mamma," I said, walking into the library room.

Mamma was lyin' on the couch, fast asleep, Mrs. Castleberry's record player on the small table beside her. The big book Doctor Prout gave her was on the floor, open. Her hand was hanging down, touching the part of the inscription that said, "Ever after, Prout." So's not to wake her, I lifted the needle off the record like it was made of felt. I crept into her bedroom and got my Daddy's bathrobe and went back and covered her with it so she wouldn't get a chill from the damp.

Time I got up to bed, it was full night. I could still hear voices laughing down the road. Harper was whining after some live thing in the bushes. I could tell Lizzy's mamma was fooling with the radio dial next door, 'cause the stations kept changing from music to talking to music again. I felt no breeze. Just damp, heavy damp. Felt like animal eyes—deer, owls, tigers—were shining at me from off the horse chestnut tree outside: Mrs. Castleberry in her hospital bed, waiting for her son; Doctor Prout running to a plane, hoping to see his mamma alive; Mamma, dreaming her happily ever after; the Contessa and Old Doctor Castleberry, who shouldn't have loved her on their mountaintop; plaster saints who didn't make miracles; a man and a woman whose faces I couldn't see, sounding like they were saying good-bye forever. They were all singing to each other in the dark, so close together they could hear the others' hearts beat. I wanted to tell them, to let them know, "My heart is beating, too. It's beating in time like yours."

Chapter Nineteen

Time I opened my eyes, the ringing had stopped. It was still dark, but just, when the night sounds go quiet and a body can hear Mr. O'Dell down the road start up his milk truck for the morning deliveries.

Mamma shuffled up the stairs. I sat up, knowing already.

"She died," I said.

My voice sounded like a light switched off.

Mamma sat on the bed beside me. She took my hands in hers. We were still as stone, like the concrete statues in the cemetery where Lizzy and I used to play hide and seek.

"That was Father Carriere," she said finally.

I pulled my hands away from hers, hugged my legs so's my chin touched my knees. I closed my eyes, but couldn't erase the sight of Mrs. Castleberry's feet gone floppy yesterday.

"She died in her sleep just after four. The hospital called. Father's got Mass this morning, so he's asked Mr. Sharp to meet Prout's plane."

Mr. Sharp was the Negro graduated from Navy officer school Mr. Owens took on after he fired Mr. Cowles for "improper use of a vehicle." His wife Cassie did the heavy cleaning for Mrs. Haldecott, who told me Cassie was expectin' a baby come any day.

Mamma pulled her belt tighter through its loops on my Daddy's hospital bathrobe. She breathed long, deep breaths so her breasts rose and dipped, rose and dipped, regular as music to a metronome. Mrs. Castleberry was layin' flat somewhere. Never'd breathe again. Right now, Doctor Prout was in the air. His own mamma dead and he didn't know.

Mamma let out a long, "Oh-hhh" sound, low like Tad's cello.

I closed my eyes, imagined Doctor Prout stepping off the plane in a little while. Mr. Sharp would see him, wave his chauffeur hat, go pick up the suitcase. Doctor Prout would nod, say, "How is she?" and Mr. Sharp would have to tell him, gentle as he could, "I'm sorry, sir, but your mother has passed over."

I flung the covers off me. Pockets of air big as balloons burst up and out my chest. Big sobs I couldn't help.

"Orla."

Mamma held me close.

"Now, now," she said, like when I had the croup, and she rubbed my back.

But Mrs. Castleberry, who just yesterday had showed me everything, was dead. The balloons split like someone sliced them with a knife. My face was wet with tears. She had only been thirsty and now she was dead.

Mr. O'Dell's truck stopped outside. The bottle of milk clinked onto the front steps. Then he walked back to the truck and, with a rumble like a low growl, was gone.

Time hiccups had replaced my crying, morning lit the sleeping porch and Mamma's hands slid from my back. I was sweaty and tired, my curls falling over my eyes. I wiped my nose with the palm of my hand and Mamma didn't try to stop me. She just kept looking at me while she stood up tall.

"Come on now, we've no time to waste. Prout will be home soon and I wouldn't be surprised if Miss Yvette gets in by this evening. We've got to get the house ready. They mustn't come home to an empty place."

Chapter Twenty

First thing Mamma did was phone Mrs. Phelps.

"Two dozen eggs, a large ham, two chickens for roasting, green beans, yams, flour, butter, two pounds of shrimp, lettuce, tomatoes, and cucumbers. Anything else I can pick up later."

We had no sooner unlocked Mrs. Castleberry's kitchen door when the Phelps' Grocery truck pulled up and Mrs. Phelps herself got out. She stayed with Mamma the whole morning, the two of them cooking like the Castleberry kitchen was a restaurant and they were preparing for the weekend buffet.

Mamma had told me to pack my good clothes for when we would serve dinner.

"I imagine Father Carriere will come. We'll use everything formal, just the way Mrs. Castleberry did for her husband."

I set the table for three in the dining room, remembering to space the silverware just the way Mrs. Castleberry taught me. Wrote place cards out, too—Miss Yvette, Doctor Prout,

Reverend Carriere. Even with the salad plates and two goblets each, the crystal fruit bowl filled with oranges, lemons, and limes in the center, the table looked lonely. Mrs. Castleberry's spot was empty. I pulled out her chair, the one with the arms and back tall enough to lean my head on, and sat down. I wouldn't have if she were still alive. But now it felt as close to her as I could get.

The screen door opened and closed in the kitchen.

"Bye, now, thanks," Mamma said.

Mrs. Phelps backed out the driveway and into the road. Pretty soon the house was quiet again. Just Mamma closing cabinet doors and wiping pots at the sink.

"Orla," she called, "Why don't you get ready? You can use Mrs. Castleberry's bathroom."

I went into the kitchen to pick up my satchel. A cool breeze rattled the screen door. Mamma sat down at the kitchen table with a glass of iced tea. She pulled her hair back into a pony tail and slipped out of her shoes. Her apron had smudges of egg on it. Even though she had worked all morning, she looked pretty.

"Want some?" she asked.

I sat down across from her. Before I could answer, the phone rang. Mamma picked it up, listened to a loud voice sounded like a lady's.

"He is?" Mamma said.

She let her pony tail drop.

"Yes, thank you for letting me know."

Mamma 'bout pulled off her clothes right in the kitchen.

"Prout's on his way. He's with Father Carriere and Mr. Charbonneau now. That was Father's secretary wondering if we were here yet."

126

Mamma turned on the shower in the maid's room, where Mrs. Patrick used to clean up before guests. Looked like she was runnin' a race.

"Go, now, hurry," she said.

She rubbed the top of my head with her knuckles.

She closed the bathroom door. She was humming, happy, like she was going to a party instead of a wake.

I walked upstairs into Mrs. Castleberry's bedroom had a little bathroom just for her. White as the dining room tablecloth, with just one pink rose in a vase. Her slippers, pink, as well, right outside the shower stall, like they were waiting for her to step into them. On the shelf above the sink that looked like a seashell, a silver picture frame with a snip of somebody's hair tied with a blue ribbon. I picked it up. "Prout's first haircut," her handwriting said. I put it back. Next to it a porcelain box in the shape of a heart. I opened it. A baby tooth. Must have been his, too. A second box, square and silver, with a clasp. I pulled it open and found a ring and a gift card, small, like ones that come from the florist.

"To Orla," it said, in her writing, "with love."

My hands trembled. I put on the ring. It slid down my finger. Fit just right. It was green, like her earrings she called "citrine." I held my hand up to the mirror. The ring sparkled. In the reflection behind me, on the little table with her face towels Mamma had folded, a perfume bottle said Arpege.

I turned, picked up the bottle, and sprayed the perfume into the room. I breathed deep, felt it mist around me, saw Mrs. Castleberry's silky nightdress on its hanger, and rubbed it between my thumb and fingers like I used to my baby blanket.

"Orla," Mamma called from downstairs. "Are you ready?"

I wasn't. Didn't want to be. Everything was changing.

127

Where would I come to after school? How would Mamma earn enough money? What if I forgot my French?

I twisted the ring round and round my finger, stripped, washed myself with Mrs. Castleberry's scented soap, then reached into my satchel and put on my first-day-of-school dress and fancy shoes used to belong to one of the Haldecott girls.

Downstairs coffee was percolating and I smelled popovers in the oven. Outside Mrs. Castleberry's window, the gravel crunched under somebody's tires.

"Here I come," I called downstairs.

I leaned out the bedroom window to the driveway. Mamma was already outside. Her hair was in a chignon and she wore the turquoise linen dress Miss Yvette had sent her when I got my paints. She stood by the picnic table, one hand resting on it, like she was posing for one of those magazines Mrs. Castleberry collected showing "Minerva Gleason at Home."

Mr. Sharp got out from the driver's seat, tipped his hat at Mamma, came around the jeep, then opened the door on the passenger side. I took in a breath.

A man looked like he had to unfold himself from the seat stepped tall into the sun. He wore sunglasses, a light blue suit, and carried a doctor's bag in his hand. He saw Mamma and let the bag fall.

"Prout," she said.

He took the glasses off and tried to put them in his suit jacket pocket, but they fell. Mamma moved to pick them up, but he stopped her, put his hand on her arm.

"I'm sorry," she said.

She had to look up at his face.

"Yes," he answered, his voice as new to me as school shoes in September, the leather kind you need to wear a while before they feel comfortable.

Then Doctor Prout wrapped his arms around my Mamma and they cried, taking no notice that Mr. Sharp had put the suitcase on the grass and was pulling out the drive.

They looked like a picture already taken. I stared down at them from Mrs. Castleberry's room, as empty as her slippers. Nothing for me to do up here, so I smoothed my dress and started downstairs, careful not to fall, taking one step at a time.

PART TWO

Chapter Twenty-One

"Here, let me help you."

Doctor Prout lifted the coffee urn out of the sink and carried it to the counter.

Wasn't much past seven, but Mamma wanted everything to be ready for when people came back to the house after the funeral. She and I had walked up from our place before six. We hadn't gotten to bed until nearly midnight both Thursday and Friday nights. No sooner had Doctor Prout arrived from Boston Thursday afternoon than Father Carriere came by, followed by Rev. and Mrs. Makepeace for a spell, and just as they were leaving, Tad's daddy with Mrs. Castleberry's death certificate and some legal papers. Was nearly ten o'clock by the time Miss Yvette got dropped off from the airport by Earl Sharp. Even then, Doctor Prout came out from his daddy's study only for a little while.

On Friday, a parade of folks marched through to plan the funeral. First Mr. Brochu with his book of hymns, next the florist to drop off flowers for the dining room and the parlor. Cassie Sharp, pregnant as she was and breathing hard from the walk, brought homemade beignets from Mrs. Haldecott. Mr. Patrick pruned the plants each side of the house and Mamma and I kept feeding everybody and making pot after pot of coffee.

Just about got to say "I'm sorry for your loss" to Doctor Prout like Mamma'd told me to when the phone started ringing for him. He took notes every call on a little pad he kept in his breast pocket, unscrewing his pen top off with his mouth, then jotting down the caller's name. After a while he just left the pad on the phone table.

"Mrs. Haldecott. Thank her for beignets," "Sam will send shrimp," "Ursuline convent offers condolences."

When Mamma introduced me, "Prout, this is Orla Gwen," he had looked at me funny, like he couldn't quite place me, and said in a deep, serious voice, "Thank you. So you are Orla, are you? Thank you."

His hand felt big and gentle on my head and he was taking snapshots of me with his eyes.

The coffee in the regular pot started to perk.

"Good," Doctor Prout said, as he looked to the stove.

I climbed off the stool, went over to turn down the burner, then came back to count out twelve scoops for the urn. I climbed onto the stool again, holding the coffee can close to my chest so it wouldn't fall, then reached over to where he had set the urn, looked at Doctor Prout and said, "Thank you, that was a help."

On the stool, I was tall as him. He was wearing his bathrobe and I caught myself staring. Curly cinnamon hair grew right out from his chest over the V of his robe. My stomach fluttered. I looked at the floor, but his feet were bare, too. One of his little toes curled in over the one next to it the way mine did on my left foot. I felt mine moving up and down, up and down, inside my sneakers. Nervousness

131

going all through my body. My hands shook a little and some coffee grounds sprinkled the counter.

"Orla, your turn."

I put the top on the urn, plugged in the cord, and climbed down again. Mamma walked out of Mrs. Patrick's room next to the pantry.

"Good Morning," Doctor Prout said.

Mamma had steam-ironed the black linen Mrs. Haldecott lent her. She had on heels with no stockings, and her legs were tan and shiny with lotion. She had pinned a short mantilla to her chignon, held her white gloves in her hands.

"Lovely," Doctor Prout said, his voice crackly.

Mamma smiled without showing her teeth and was about to speak when the phone rang and Miss Yvette picked up in the foyer.

"For you, of course," she clicked into the kitchen and lifted her eyes to Prout as she took the cup of coffee Mamma had just poured for her. Prout went to the phone.

Miss Yvette looked just like *Life Magazine* pictures of Mrs. Kennedy. Her dress skimmed her body so she made the letter A in black. A small hat sat right in the center of her honey hair came just down to her chin. For the first time ever nothing on her jangled. A white handkerchief peeked out from between the black lace gloves she carried.

Doctor Prout came in again just as Mr. Patrick shuffled up the steps to the back door using a cane looked like the top was made of pearl.

"The car's ready," he said to Mamma, mopping his forehead with a handkerchief looked just-ironed.

I noticed for the first time that all the lines on his face pointed down.

Mamma put on her gloves.

"No," said Doctor Prout.

He spoke sharp, like he was giving an order.

Miss Yvette raised her eyebrows at him, opened her mouth to speak, then didn't. Mr. Patrick eased himself down onto one of the chairs by the table and put his handkerchief into his breast pocket. Mamma got him a glass of water.

His voice softened, "That was Sheriff Powell. He's sending one of his deputies to escort us. It appears my mother has decided to provide us with a memorable funeral. She has upset the Klan. They are already at St. Marguerite's."

Doctor Prout's voice shook a little when he said, "my mother," and he cracked his knuckles, one hand at a time. I shivered in the heat. The church had just got repaired from after the fair. Took most of June to replace the stained glass windows. I brushed my arm, remembered the gun touching it. Rubbed my fingers together, feeling the ashes used to be my paintings. My stomach grabbed inside and I felt the color leaving my face. Mamma put her hands on my shoulders.

"Orla," she said, the way she did when the dentist had been ready to pull out the baby molar that hurt, the way that meant, "Don't make a fuss. You're a big girl now."

Mr. Patrick twisted his cane around and around on the linoleum. He rubbed his face with his other hand. Looked up at Mamma.

"My daughter can look after her, Minerva. She doesn't have to go."

Mamma knelt in front of me. She stroked my cheek.

"What do you want to do?" she asked.

I put my hand on hers. The side of my neck was pounding. Everyone was looking at me. I thought of Mrs. Castleberry last Easter, how she had pretended not to be afraid of Mr. Cowles when she helped Reverend Makepeace get Spencer into the house. That she had said my name before Sheriff Powell drove her away. How on purpose I had sprayed her Arpege so some of it would mist over me.

I pressed her citrine ring hard against my finger with my thumb so I could say the words I didn't mean.

"Well?" Mamma said.

Miss Yvette drank down her coffee all at once and carried her cup to the sink. She stood by the screen door and snapped her gloves back and forth on her hand.

I took in a breath and said what Mrs. Castleberry would have wanted.

"I'd rather go. I want to go, Mamma."

I didn't dare blink or say another word, just kept my eyes open and stared straight ahead. Mamma stood up. I fixed my eyes on the creases had formed on her dress from her kneeling. They made gashes left and right from her waist to her knees.

"I'd best get dressed," said Doctor Prout, and Mamma nudged me toward Mrs. Patrick's room to get out of my pedal pushers and into my Easter dress she had turned into a funeral outfit. The pink ribbons were black now and she had sewn in a black tulle underskirt cut from one of Mrs. Haldecott's old ball gowns.

As I was slipping into my shoes, I heard two cars pull into the driveway. I looked out the window and saw Deputy Smith get out of his cruiser while Mr. Hedge, the funeral parlor owner, opened the doors to the limousine. Miss Yvette went right over to him and Mr. Hedge tipped his hat, then helped her into the back seat. Mr. Patrick followed, struggling into the front seat across from where Mr. Hedge would be driving. Had to lift his right leg with his hand. Then he leaned out the door and reached to the ground to pick up his cane that had dropped.

"Ready?" Mamma asked, knocking on the door.

I looked into the mirror, pinched my cheeks to try and make them pink, then made the sign of the cross that none of us would get hurt. Guillotine, guillotine, guillotine repeated in my mind.

End of the school year, Tad had been studying the French Revolution and made a miniature guillotine that really worked. One day he peeled some bananas and dropped the blade over and over again until mounds of banana slices piled up on the floor.

"Round as heads," Billy Carroll had laughed.

I gagged, tasted the cornflakes I'd eaten for breakfast, then said, "Yes," came out, and looked to Mamma.

She nodded at how I looked, wrinkled her nose, and said, "I see you found my lotion, too."

The black tulle scratched my legs and I tried to think about that instead of what could happen.

Mr. Hedge put Mamma and me in the seat that felt like a couch across from Miss Yvette. Miss Yvette held her legs together just like Mrs. Castleberry used to, and I tried not to stare.

Doctor Prout came out of the house and got in beside his aunt. Deputy Smith came over and leaned into the car to talk to him.

"I'll lead you, Prout. Mr. Hedge will follow. Don't none of you get out of the car until we tell you. Be sure you follow our instructions. The hearse is already there."

Doctor Prout adjusted himself in his seat.

"Yes, sir," he said, "We'll do as you say."

Mr. Hedge closed the door beside Doctor Prout. The limousine smelled just vacuumed. I knew nobody could see through its darkened windows. But they didn't have to. Everbody'd know it was us.

Chapter Twenty-Two

Nobody spoke. Felt like we were all inside Mrs. Castleberry's black velvet jewelry case. We rounded the bend into town. Katie Cowles was skipping rope in her yard. Cassie Sharp rested against the side of Carroll's store to watch us pass. Mr. Carroll, coming out the door in a suit said he'd be coming to church, saluted as we drove by. Looked like an ordinary day. But my finger nails dug red lines into my palms.

The limousine glided to a stop behind Deputy Smith's car in front of St. Marguerite's. The pall bearers were already carrying Mrs. Castleberry's casket into the church. Right across the road from us stood two lines of men in white gowns and pointy hoods. Their faces were covered with white flaps, and I could see their hands crossed like X's in front of them. They looked all the same except for their shoes. One man had shiny black-laced ones, another two farmer boots, a fourth, must have been Mr. Wills from the box factory, wearin' his usual pointy-toed cowboy boots with the green swirls, another white bucks, and one more a pair of sneakers.

Four wooden sawhorses they could tip over by just pushing if they wanted to made a straight line in front of them. Standing in the middle of the road was Sheriff Powell and three other men dressed like Tad's daddy did when he went hunting. All four were carrying rifles. Sheriff didn't have on his usual broad-brimmed hat, but a helmet instead, like the others.

He walked toward the limousine while the other three stood facing the white hoods, and Mr. Hedge cranked his window down.

"Morning," Sheriff said.

He pulled a dark-glass visor up so we could see his face. Bullet-proof, must have been. I rubbed my eyes. Only Doctor Prout had sunglasses. Out the window to my left I saw the rectory door open and Father Carriere came out with Tad and Billy Carroll holding the big candles. The white hoods began to hum in one voice sounded like an engine idling.

"The archbishop and the nigger minister are already inside," said the sheriff, leaning in to see Doctor Prout.

Mr. Patrick groaned in the front seat. "Nigger" echoed in my head.

"Archbishop Rummel?" Mamma said.

Only time he ever came was for Confirmation.

"This is ridiculous, Prout. If I had known this would become a spectacle," said Miss Yvette, "I'd have insisted you bring her to New York."

She folded her arms across her chest and stared at the hoods across the street. Doctor Prout tried to put his arm around her, but she shoved him away. He put his hands together and cracked his knuckles, looking down at them.

"Okay, Orla," Mamma said.

Mr. Hedge had gotten out, come around and was opening the door. Doctor Prout stepped out first, turned back to help his aunt, who waved his hand away and got out herself. Then Mr. Hedge reached in to me. Mamma pushed me toward him, then got out right behind me, folding me into herself as we walked into church. Her chin rested on my head. Her heart beat on my back. We were like those Russian dolls that fit into each other in Mrs. Castleberry's living room.

We followed Father Carriere, Tad, and Billy right behind Miss Yvette and Doctor Prout. Mr. Hedge helped Mr. Patrick behind us.

"Easy, now, Mr. Patrick. Nice and easy."

I could hear him puffing.

The organ played loud. The choir was singing, "For all the saints/Who from their labors rest," but the hum still carried from across the street.

"Nig-ger lov-ers, Nig-ger lov-ers, Nig-ger love-ers, Nig-..."

"Don't turn around," Mamma said, as she guided me shaking up the steps and into the church.

The double church doors banged shut behind us and I jumped. Deputy Smith stood in front of them with his finger on the trigger. I turned back toward the procession and watched Archibishop Rummel meet Mrs. Castleberry's casket halfway down the aisle. He put his hand on top a moment, then turned and walked ahead to the altar.

Mr. Hedge led Miss Yvette and Doctor Prout to the first row on the left side. Then he pointed for Mamma and me to go toward the right. We let Mr. Patrick go in first, then Mamma got in, so I'd be on the aisle. We stood until the music stopped and Father Carriere motioned for us all to sit down.

Right up on the altar to the left of the marble consecration table sat Reverend and Mrs. Makepeace, Cassie Sharp's neighbor who was supposed to have magical powers, and another Negro lady I saw once hanging clothes outside

Mrs. Allaire's house. Reverend Makepeace was wearing his minister collar instead of a tie, and the ladies were dressed in choir robes the same color as the Blessed Virgin's blue cape over on the side altar. They had on lace gloves just like Miss Yvette's, only theirs were white.

"*In nomine Patris, et Filii, at Spiritus Sancti,*" Father began.

Words and music floated around me. I felt myself moving like I was supposed to with the prayers, but didn't think, just followed along the way a leaf might on the river. My eyes were drawn instead to Mrs. Castleberry's casket. If I reached out my left arm I could have touched it. It was mahogany, just like her dining room table, and almost as big. There were silver handles on the side for the pall bearers. White calla lilies lay on top, and the tall Easter candle flickered over them. Mrs. Castleberry would be very small inside, like a doll that could break in a beautiful box. I hoped somebody had made sure her feet didn't get left flopped. That her hair was combed and she was dressed like she'd be going to lunch at The Links. I closed my eyes and saw the clear polish on her fingernails, "short enough to play without making distracting clicking sounds," she had said every piano lesson we had.

I was leaning on the arm of the pew staring at her and imagining her favorite piece to play, "In a Persian Market," when Mamma whispered, "Stand up now, Orla, the Gospel."

The whir of the ceiling fans moved the air so Archbishop Rummel's vestments fluttered as he stood up and crossed from his chair to the pulpit to read the Gospel. I didn't notice the words so much as his voice. Just like he was reading us a story. He had been born in Germany, Mrs. Castleberry told me one time. Now, without his miter on, he looked like somebody's granddaddy.

"My good people," he said, his arms reaching out to the whole church, "we have heard the Word of the Lord."

"Good" was "goot," "we" was "ve", "word" was "verd."

He motioned for us to sit down as he arranged two or three papers on the pulpit. I felt Mrs. Carroll's fan back and forth behind my neck. The windows were open, but it was quiet outside. I looked back to make sure Deputy Smith was still at the door. The archbishop cleared his throat. On the altar, Tad smoothed down his hair and Billy crossed and uncrossed his feet. Reverend Makepeace wiped his face with a handkerchief. The Negro ladies folded their gloved hands on their laps. The air hung heavy with the fragrance of calla lilies and pink roses.

"I met Belle Castleberry by accident, you might say," the archbishop began.

He smiled. So did Father Carriere.

"I had taken a fall while hiking some thirteen years ago, and Bellefleur's husband, Old Doctor Castleberry, as I understand he is fondly remembered, operated on my broken leg."

The archbishop looked down at Doctor Prout, who nodded up at the pulpit. I heard whispering farther back in the church.

"We had occasion to discuss many matters each time he paid me a house call, and one day, he invited me to dinner. So I first met Bellefleur Castleberry when she welcomed me into her home."

I looked over to Mamma.

"Did you...?" I asked.

She motioned no and whispered, "Mrs. Patrick was still alive."

From that evening on, we kept in touch. As many of you know, Belle was already well known in New Orleans for her generosity to the Ursuline Academy," he motioned out into the pew behind Doctor Prout and Miss Yvette, where a group of nuns sat, heads bowed as he pointed toward them.

"After her husband's death, we continued to share a supper a few times a year, and in 1953 when I wrote my pastoral letter condemning segregation, she became one of my foremost critics, believing as she did for so long in maintaining the racial and socio-economic status quo in our parishes."

"He should have listened to her," Mr. Patrick muttered to Mamma.

Mamma patted his knee and he rubbed his hand across his mouth. There was rustling in the pews behind us. On the altar, if he had heard, Reverend Makepeace gave no sign. He, his wife, Cassie Sharp's magician neighbor, and the other Negro lady just kept their eyes on the archbishop, who went onto the second page of his sermon.

"Two years ago Belle was diagnosed with heart trouble. She kept her illness from nearly everyone and asked me to become her spiritual advisor and confessor as she prepared for death. I agreed."

Somebody sneezed.

"She spent a great deal of time reading and re-reading the words I had written, then agreed to help a Negro priest perfect his French so he could work more effectively as the chaplain for an order of French nuns."

I wondered if Mrs. Castleberry had made him sit in the kitchen or if she brought him into the parlor.

"And over time, she experienced a change of heart. So interestingly, perhaps even miraculously, over the past few months she and I have worked on a committee that will see our Catholic schools integrated in September."

I heard a kneeler slam in the back and Mr. Ouellette's voice said right out loud, "Over my dead body."

The archbishop ignored him.

"In fact, a few months ago in April, Belle sought my approval to visit Mrs. Gaillot, an excommunicant like Mr. Perez and Mr. Ricau, to try to convince her of the justice of my decision. She wrote me of her failed attempt: 'Your Excellency, On arriving at the Gaillot residence, I rang the bell at the front door. A maid met me and directed me to come around to the back. I did so, where the same maid asked me to wait. Mrs. Gaillot came to the door and asked me my business. When I implored her to join forces with us, she called me a messenger from Satan and slammed the door.'"

The archbishop had to wait for the whispering and muttering to stop before he could continue reading.

"'Your Excellency, that experience was a revelation, a mortifying one at that. *Mon Dieu*, how many times have I met others at my own back door? Unaware, unconvinced that there should be another way?'"

Mamma looked at Mr. Patrick. He turned to her and clasped her arm. They both stared up at the archbishop.

"I suggested to Belle that she and I make our prayer our journey together in Christ by reading the prayers of the fourteenth-century mystic Julian of Norwich, like Belle a formidable woman of her own time. By Belle's own estimation, the words of Julian reverberated in her and, as she put it in a letter to me just a few weeks before her death, 'are healing my spiritual heart just as the physical organ is shriveling inside me.'"

Miss Yvette made a small sound, then put one of her hands to her mouth. Doctor Prout put his arm around her. Archbishop Rummel took a handkerchief from under his robes and patted his forehead. He looked at Doctor Prout and Miss Yvette for a long time. Then he wet his lips and looked from the pulpit down over Mrs. Castleberry's casket to us. He locked his eyes on Mamma and me.

"'The sin of my life has been thinking myself in charge, of misguided love,' she wrote me. 'As death approaches, I will atone for that sin the best I can.' Then she shared a translation of Julian's words that she believed spoke directly to her. I pass these words along to you. Think of them as we lay God's beloved Belle Dubois Castleberry to rest. Think of them as we examine our own failings. Think of them as each of us opens our own hearts to make our parishes, this parish, home to all who seek it, as Belle learned it must be:

'Loving Father,
I bring to you all my faults
And especially my wrath.
I see my anger leads to a dreadful failing,
A shameful falling,
And a sorrowful dying.
But in this dying
I trust your mercy
Continually at work protecting me
Even against myself,
And turning everything to good for us.

In the end everything will be love.'

Let us pray."

Mr. Patrick let go of Mamma and put his head in his hands, and I felt my heart thumping hard inside me. I looked at Mamma as we stood for the Offertory. Her cheeks were wet, her face flushed. Mr. Brochu was singing "Ave Maria" and I felt myself disappearing into the music. Mrs. Castleberry's operas started playing in my head. I felt red and pulsing, full and hungry at the same time. Then we were kneeling, the pews were squeaking around me. I wanted to see her again. But I knew I wouldn't. Ever. I felt myself crying out loud, and Mamma was rubbing my back. I looked at the casket, breathed in the flowers, remembered it was me she wanted last. I heard my own sobs. Over the casket, Doctor Prout's eyes reached mine.

"Domine, non sum dignus ut intres sub tectum meum: sed tantum dic verbo et sanabitur anima mea."

We stood for the procession to the altar. Two long lines shuffling. The Body of Christ. Amen, amen, amen.

Time everybody received Communion and settled down in the pews, a baby whimpered way back, and the pall bearers, led by Mr. Hedge, came down the aisle and stood on both sides of the casket.

Archbishop Rummel motioned to Tad for his miter, then he, Father Carriere, Tad, and Billy came around the altar table and stood on the steps by the Easter candle. Reverend Makepeace and the Negro ladies stood behind them in a row, one step up. Archbishop Rummel turned and nodded to Reverend Makepeace.

"Friends," he said, and stretched out his arms.

"The nerve," Mrs. Allaire blurted out a few rows back.

We all turned around to see. Mrs. Allaire's son helped his mother out their pew and they walked out together, didn't even try to be quiet.

"Friends," Reverend Makepeace repeated.

My neck stiffened. I looked again. Deputy Smith made the Allaire's wait at the door, motioning with his rifle. Mr. Allaire slapped his arm. He didn't budge.

"Gentlemen," Mr. Hedge said.

I turned back as the pallbearers reached for the silver handles.

The archbishop moved up to stand with Reverend Makepeace. The ceiling fans whirred. I felt faint, sat down. Mamma rubbed my back some more.

Reverend Makepeace continued, "Bellefleur Dubois Castleberry has gone home to Our Lord and Savior. May He forgive her her sins and imperfections, recognize her desire to do good in this world, and reward her for her many acts of kindness to those closest to her and those from whom she might have turned."

He came down the steps and went over to Doctor Prout and Miss Yvette. But he still spoke so everyone could hear:

"Please accept my sympathies on the loss of your mother and your sister. She was a friend to me and my congregation. She was teaching us to see the White community in a new way. May others follow her example."

Kneelers slammed. "Nigger" more than once from the pews. I stood up straight, grabbed hold of Mamma's hand.

Doctor Prout and the reverend shook hands. Miss Yvette gave him a quick nod. Mr. Patrick tapped his cane on the floor. Then Father Carriere motioned up to Mr. Brochu.

"May the Angels lead her to Paradise and may she rest in peace," the organist sang.

Archbishop, priest, and minister made the sign of the cross over her casket, the pall bearers turned on their heels, and Mr. Hedge led the procession out as the choir sang "Now Thank We All Our God." Tad looked quick at me as he passed, and Mamma and I held Mr. Patrick between us as we followed behind Archbishop Rummel, Father Carriere, the Negroes, Doctor Prout, Miss Yvette, and the five nuns.

Chapter Twenty-Three

Deputy Smith had opened the doors, but still stood guard while people walked into the sun. Father Carriere, Doctor Prout and Miss Yvette stayed inside by the holy water font shaking hands with the crowd. Mr. Patrick rested on the steps leading to the choir loft. A few steps away from him, where I could hear the hum starting again, Archbishop Rummel stopped by Mamma and me.

"Your Excellency," Mamma said, and bowed to kiss his big purple ring.

I curtsied, the way the pictures showed in Mamma's King Arthur book.

"Belle told me all about you both," he said.

Mamma's face turned into an empty canvas. She didn't speak, kept her lips closed tight together. I waited, listening to the hum, getting nervous about going outside.

"Be assured," he spoke to Mamma like he was her friend. "Be assured, Minerva. As Julian herself told us, 'All will be well.'"

He put his hands on Mamma's shoulders, made a cross on her forehead. Then he smiled, a big, happy smile, right at Mamma. Her eyes filled up and she nodded to him like she understood something he meant. She ruffled my hair and tried to smile, too, but instead tears ran down her face.

Archbishop Rummel took her hand, then whispered in my ear, "You will paint her, yes? She wrote me you are an artist. Let me know when you are ready to show me the portrait."

My heart leapt. Of course I'd paint her! But before I could answer him, he turned and left us, striding into the sun outside.

Mamma and I followed, stopping just inside the doors to the church as he walked down the steps. He turned to face everyone on the steps beneath us, made a big sign of the cross, then waved good-bye and walked toward the Owens' jeep. Earl Sharp in his chauffeur's uniform held the door open. His face looked like a statue, but his right foot tapped fast, up and down on the pavement. Across the road, I saw the three guards facing the hooded men, holding their rifles ready. All of a sudden, something red flew from one of the white robes and burst on the archbishop's miter. Then two more rotten tomatoes, till Archbishop Rummel was dripping red.

The guards pushed the sawhorses back into the white robes with their bodies and pointed their guns at the hooded men.

"Think," the archbishop hollered across the roof of the jeep to them, "think what you are doing!"

"Nigger-loving bastard!" one of the robes shouted while the others cheered.

The archbishop disappeared into the jeep and Earl Sharp got himself into the driver's seat from the passenger side. He started the engine, then skidded out into the road. More rotten tomatoes splattered on the road just short of the jeep as it went.

The guards poked the hooded men with their rifles. Doctor Prout just about carried Miss Yvette to the limousine. He came back up the steps for Mamma and me. Crouched over both of us as we walked. I was so angry I felt like getting hold of one of Tad's old grenades and hurling it right into those men so mean but wouldn't show their faces.

"Bastards," I heard my voice say. Loud. Its own live thing.

No one corrected me, or even minded. That made me angrier still. Like it didn't matter. Like it wasn't just a bad word, or me not bein' ladylike, but the truth. The plain, horrible, disgusting truth.

The robed men started goin' their own ways. Doctor Prout went back into the church to get Mr. Patrick. Sheriff took off his helmet and watched the white robes disappear, some toward town, others away from it.

"He won't come," Doctor Prout said, getting into the limousine himself. "Says he wants to speak with Father Carriere."

We waited for Mr. Hedge, who was standin' by the hearse. Miss Yvette looked like paste.

When only a couple of men were left across the road, Sheriff Powell and the three guards walked into the church, then came out right away with Reverend Makepeace and the Negro ladies Deputy Smith had told to stay inside. They walked them over to the reverend's car was parked next to Father's by the rectory. Tad and Billy followed, carryin' their altar-boy clothes over their arms. Billy slipped on some of the splattered tomatoes, but Tad caught him before he fell. He looked at the ground and, all of a sudden, his face got serious. I knew he was figuring out what had happened. He stooped down by the dark windows to look into the limousine. Waved like he could see us anyway.

Mr. Hedge got into the driver's seat. He left his door open while he wiped something wet off his shoes.

"See you bowling, then," one of the last two hooded men said to the other, walking right by the limousine.

"Yessir," the one in sneakers answered, shakin' his hand. "Next Tuesday, right?"

Mr. Hedge closed the door.

"Well then," he said.

I felt a big breath ease out my chest.

"We'll take her to the cemetery privately after things quiet down," said Doctor Prout. "They'll hold her at the funeral home until then."

Miss Yvette wrinkled her eyebrows at him, put her handkerchief to her lips, and wept.

"Belle," she said, as we pulled away from the church. "Oh, Belle."

Chapter Twenty-Four

Mrs. Haldecott was the last to leave. Time she stood up from her rocker and brushed the macaroon crumbs off her dress the church bells were ringing five o'clock. I was collectin' tablecloths and napkins from the front yard and counting whatever silver had been left there and on the veranda. Me and Mamma had most all the dishes washed, the coffee and tea cups were turned upside down and lined up on cotton dishtowels along the kitchen counters. Nothing was left in the coffee urn but the grounds Mamma had me throw right into the vegetable garden by the potting shed. The ham bone pretty well picked over on the big platter would be the start of pea soup next week. Sympathy cards still in their envelopes piled up on the phone table in the foyer, and the front yard was littered with cookies that got dropped, a few soggy tea napkins, and some glasses of champagne punch part way full.

Miss Yvette still had her hat on, but she was barefoot now, and her hot-pink toenails didn't match her face. She usually asked the kinds of questions that kept a conversation going—"Tell me, now, Libby, what has your oldest son decided to do after he graduates?" or "How do you compare your sister's experience abroad last summer to your own, Marie, that year you studied in Paris?" But right after Father Carriere left for confessions just after four, she had stretched herself out on one of the chaise lounges and pretty much but stared into the yard, hardly talking at all.

"Prout," said Mrs. Haldecott, standing up to go, her hand on the veranda rail to steady her, "you just call me when you're ready to come to supper before you go back to Boston. You and Yvette plan to spend a relaxing evening with me. I'll have Cassie make more beignets. We'll sit in the gazebo on the dock and reminisce. Lord, I am going to miss your mother so."

She waved her hand across her face like she was brushin' something out of her eyes, then bent down to kiss Doctor Prout on the top of his head.

Doctor Prout let her, then lifted himself out from the rocker he had draped his suit jacket over. He towered over her, and Mrs. Haldecott had to tilt her head all the way back to look at his face. His white shirt was a mess of wrinkles except where he had rolled the sleeves. One end of his bow tie was sticking out his breast pocket, and he blew his nose on the handkerchief had his blue monogram.

"Thank you, Ma'am, thank you. Yes, we'll certainly call, right Tante Yvette?"

Miss Yvette sorta jumped, then turned her head toward the both of them.

"I'm sorry," she said, sitting up straighter, "I'm afraid I've forgotten myself."

Mrs. Haldecott turned to face her.

"Understandable, dear. Don't you fret any, just sit right there and try to rest. We'll talk soon."

151

She held the handrail and walked down the steps, carrying in her free hand a dried flower miniature Mrs. Castleberry had made and Miss Yvette had given her as a remembrance.

Right then Mamma walked out onto the veranda from inside. I stood on the bottom step, tryin' not to drop my handfuls of forks, coffee spoons, and soiled napkins.

"Might I get anyone anything else?" she asked.

Over the dress she was wearing her ruffled company apron had mustard smudges on it. Her shoes were gone and she was wearing the sneakers she usually saved for laundry days. Her chignon was coming undone, a soggy dishtowel hung over one arm, and she wiped her forehead with the back of her hand.

"Oh, by the way, Minerva," Mrs. Haldecott said, stopping on the path just past me to look back up at Mamma, "I don't know how much longer Miss Yvette and Doctor Prout will need your services here, and with Cassie soon due to give birth, I certainly could use some help. Why don't you come by in a few days so we can agree to something."

Mamma's didn't answer. Doctor Prout turned his face toward her like he would ask a question, looked at her long, the same way he did me when we first met. But she didn't move her eyes to his, just kept facing Mrs. Haldecott on the path. I could tell from her lips tight together she was tryin' to keep something inside.

Doctor Prout looked down at Mrs. Haldecott a moment, then back to Mamma, studyin' her from top to bottom, his eyes finally fixing on her feet where her big toe peeked out from her right sneaker. Everybody was waiting for somebody else to speak.

I heard the tick tick tick of the grandfather clock by the phone table in the foyer and the whoosh of the fleur-de-lis banner on the flagpole in the garden when a hot puff of air blew up from the river. Two gray mice scurried out into the yard from under the latticework beneath the veranda. A line of ants marched across the path just below me. I felt an ugly lump growing in my throat.

Without warning, Miss Yvette sat up straight, stretched her arms high, and flung her legs out from the chaise lounge.

"I could use a Scotch," she said, louder than she had to.

She stood up and took three hat pins from her Mrs. Kennedy hat. She turned the hat on its side and rolled it like a wheel from one hand to the other.

Mamma's chignon fell all the way out, and she turned away without sayin' good-bye and went back into the house. Doctor Prout escorted Mrs. Haldecott to her car. I brought my armful of things into the kitchen, heard Mamma flush the toilet and turn on the faucets in Mrs. Patrick's old room, and went ahead and got the bottle of Chivas we always served Father Carriere. I put two tumblers, one for Miss Yvette, one for Doctor Prout, onto a tray, filled another taller glass with ice cubes, grabbed the small ice tongs, and came back onto the veranda as Doctor Prout walked back up the steps, turned and waved to Mrs. Haldecott pulling out of the drive in her white Cadillac.

Mamma came back outside just as I was about to go back in to slice some lemons so we'd have peel shavings for the drinks, when Doctor Prout motioned to another rocker and said, "Minerva, join us, please, you've been on your feet all day. I can't thank you enough for your help."

He sounded just like Mrs. Castleberry telling Mr. Patrick to rest a spell last Christmas when he got dizzy and dropped the hors d'oeuvres tray.

Miss Yvette raised her eyebrows, said, "Excuse me a moment," then walked inside and up the stairs, still twirling her hat.

"I'll get the lemons, Mamma," I said.

I faced Doctor Prout, "Would you like some nuts, too?"

"Thank you kindly, Orla," Doctor Prout answered, but Mamma didn't seem to hear me.

I followed after Miss Yvette and walked toward the kitchen, but Mamma's voice stopped me short by the umbrella stand.

"You heard her, Prout. I am the help. I've been on nothing but my feet since high school graduation."

Mamma's sounded mean, like she was not just ordinary tired, but angry tired, too.

I stood still as I could and waited for what Doctor Prout might say. Listened to Miss Yvette's shoes thud on her bedroom floor, heard her go into the bathroom and run the water tap till it was sure to be hot, counted her steps back to her bedroom again, and listened to the desk chair scrape the floor. The bedsprings might've squeaked.

I tiptoed backwards toward the screen door again, turned around, and peered out. They were still standing there, staring at each other, hands at their sides. Doctor Prout had a look on his face seemed confused.

The clock ticked some more. I rubbed my fingers along the door frame. I didn't know what to do.

Doctor Prout cleared his throat.

"I...Minerva, I never imagined you that way. Come, sit with me."

Mamma threw back her head and laughed.

"Well, then, your imagination is lacking," she said. "Look at me."

She ran her hands down her clothes.

154

"Look what I've become. You're only asking because she's dead. You're here because she died."

Mamma pulled her apron over her face to catch her sobs.

Doctor Prout stood with his mouth open.

"Where were you before? Where were you before I hated my life?"

I heard myself gasp, covered my mouth with my hand. I felt my chest with my hand, listened for my heart. It didn't even pound. Like it had stopped to wonder why it should bother. My hands felt clammy. I wanted to disappear, to climb into the mahogany casket with Mrs. Castleberry. "Orla," she'd say, "I called you and you came."

Mamma snapped the wet dish towel on the veranda rail, then threw it to the floor between her and Doctor Prout. I crossed my arms over my chest and held myself tight. He started toward her.

"Please, Minerva," he said.

Then Mamma grabbed one of the tumblers off the tray, raised it high and hissed, "Your child is a cocktail waitress, for God's sake!" and flung the glass at one of the porch columns.

Doctor Prout jumped and a shard of glass caught him on the neck. Ice cubes flew and glass shattered on the wooden floor. A line of blood trickled onto his collar.

The lump in my throat got so big I most couldn't breathe. My eyes twitched and I held onto the door frame to keep from falling.

Doctor Prout put his hand to his throat, took it away and stared at the blood on his fingers. He stooped down and picked up the dishcloth, then tied it around his neck. Mamma watched him, her hands balled into fists.

"I'm sorry," he said. "So very sorry, Minerva."

He was crying, too.

155

The church bells chimed five-thirty. Miss Yvette picked up the phone in the hall upstairs and said, "Person-to-person call, please." I made myself breathe around the lump, one two three and in, four five six and out. Again. Again. Again.

The veranda floor creaked as Mamma shifted her weight. In slow motion she opened her hands, then walked three steps over to Doctor Prout and slapped him hard both sides of his face. He didn't even flinch. Then she threw herself at him, grabbing his shoulders hard. He wrapped his arms around her shoulders, then moved his hands, digging his red fingers into her head. He pressed so hard that her bun she had just put in place again came out, and her hair fell all around her shoulders. Their hands were everywhere there was skin. Mamma had blood on her arms and the dishcloth came undone and fell. Then Doctor Prout was kissing Mamma, holding her face close to his, and she moaned.

I pressed myself against the wall so I wouldn't scream. I held my legs together tight to stop their shaking.

"Fred," Miss Yvette said upstairs. "Yes, over now. Awful."

Doctor Prout repeated MinervaMinervaMinerva. I hated them both. I dug my nails into my arms.

Then, like she had changed her mind, Mamma pushed him away, made him stop. She stood up straight and fixed her hair again, then called into the house in a high voice, "Orla, Doctor Prout and I are going for a walk. We'll be back shortly, honey."

I held my breath, didn't answer.

Then Mamma led Doctor Prout down the steps like he needed help walking. They put their arms around each other's shoulders and walked over the grass toward the drive. I ran into the kitchen, watched out the screen door, and saw them slip behind Mrs. Castleberry's station wagon and into the potting shed. The door slammed behind them. Mamma didn't once look back.

"No!" I kicked the wall till I made black marks on the yellow paint, then rubbed the prickly tulle over top my knees till tiny bubbles of red appeared.

Upstairs, Miss Yvette said, "I'll speak to you again tomorrow. Be back as soon as I can."

I dragged my nails down the screen over and over till they became black claws.

"Prout," Miss Yvette called, "where are you?" as she walked back onto the veranda.

I could've answered, but I was already on the road the other side of the hedgerow. I took off my shoes and let the pebbles hurt the bottoms of my feet as I walked fast toward home. The road dust coated my feet and ankles and turned them dirty clay. I shook my hair to make it wild. "Hate," my lips formed the word, "hatehatehatehate," I banged my teeth together.

A car came toward me from town. Mr. Charbonneau in his convertible. He waved, then slowed down.

"Might I give you a ride, young lady?" he asked. "You look like you could use a glass of cool water and a restful night. Where's your mother?"

I tried to be myself.

"Thanks, Mr. Charbonneau, but I'll just walk. She's still up at the house. Say hi to Tad for me."

He took off his hat, put it on the seat beside him.

"You sure, now?" he said. "Everything alright? You must have had a rough day."

My lip quivered, but I just shook my head yes and started walking away. He waited a spell. I knew he was watchin' me in his rear-view mirror, so I tried to walk happier. When I got round the bend, he drove away, but slow.

The key was under the mat in the usual place, so I let myself in. I took it and put it on top of the ice box so Mamma'd be locked out when she came. I kicked my shoes under the kitchen table, pulled my dress over my head and dropped it on the floor, then practically naked got the big scissors from the drawer where we kept the glue and tape for holding pipes together and making projects for school. I carried them opposite the way I knew to so the pointy parts were sticking out in front of me like daggers.

I curled around the door into the library room to make sure the curtains were drawn. I walked in, put the scissors down on the coffee table, knelt, and pulled the King Arthur book from under the sofa. I slid it out from the pillowcase, opened to page one, then ripped every page from the spine till I got to the end. I cut them all this way and that, some into triangles, others squares. When I got tired of cutting, I shredded more by hand, till most of the pieces were small as stamps. I grabbed them in bunches and flung them all over the room. Next I opened the cover wide so it covered most of the coffee table, then I took a thick black piece of charcoal and drew L-I-A-R in big capital letters over where Doctor Prout had written "Princess" to Mamma.

A car drove by. Across the street Mrs. Carroll called, "Suppertime." A phone kept ringing far away, then finally stopped.

I climbed the stairs and walked into my bedroom, got my treasure chest from the shelf in my closet, then went out onto the sleepin' porch, and sat down on the floor. I opened the chest and lifted out the picture of Mamma and my Daddy from their wedding, then got up and put it on my pillow on the bed my Daddy made me.

I heard baseball sounds from Lizzy's radio. Cats mewed down in the alley. I was dripping sweat and hoping Mamma was scared she couldn't find me. I bent over the picture and kissed my Daddy's face.

"Lizzy," I heard Mrs. Crowther call. "If you'd like, we'll go to Sam's for supper."

I came downstairs, listened to each step creak *hate my life*, went into Mamma's room, and took my Daddy's hospital bathrobe from the closet, then locked myself in the bathroom with it. I drew a bath as hot as I could stand, sprinkled soap flakes into the tub, and eased myself in up to my neck in water. I scrubbed my arms hard as I could to get the smell of Mamma's lotion off me.

Time the bathroom got all steamed up and the air swirled like smoke out the screen high over the tub, the game had stopped next door and Lizzy and her mamma came out.

"See you there," Mrs. Crowther called out to somebody.

Pretty soon, a car drove up and stopped outside. Two doors slammed. Feet ran. All of a sudden, Mamma was pounding on the door.

"The key's gone. Orla, open up, honey. Orla, where's the key?"

I didn't answer, just let her bang while I pulled the plug out of the drain and stood up in the tub watching the bubbly water disappear, leaving traces of sand on the porcelain under my cut feet.

It got quiet. She'd have to pull out one of the screens. I looked in the mirror at myself. My hair was a nest of snakes. I put on my Daddy's robe and waited.

"There," Doctor Prout's voice said, and Mamma tumbled into the house from the window in the front hall.

"Orla!" she hollered.

She ran upstairs to my room and onto the sleeping porch. Then down the stairs toward hers.

"Orla!"

Doctor Prout stood at the front door. I walked out of the bathroom in my Daddy's hospital robe and pretended he wasn't there. I looked at Mamma coming toward me, her face moving, her eyes wide open, and yelled, "I hate you!" loud as I could.

She didn't say a word, just dragged me by my hands to her big bed. She wrapped herself around me and we fell together onto the mattress. I pummeled her breasts with my fists.

"Liar," I said, over and over into her chest.

Our tears mixed. I smelled bath soap and soil and something like sweat. His blood was on her arms. My slobber on her face. We sobbed and sobbed, hurting and holding, till finally our breath came in, went out, in and out, slow and slower still, a length of tired and sorry sighs.

I woke up just when the night insects began to saw outside and untangled myself from Mamma's arms. She didn't stir. I sat up and looked from the bed to the door. The room was all shadows, so I had to blink. Doctor Prout sat crouched on the floor, his knees to his chest, his head in his hands. The mattress squeaked when I moved, and he lifted his head. He leaned it against the doorframe, one side of him in Mamma's room, the other side out. Waiting like me to see which of us she would choose.

Chapter Twenty-Five

First thing I smelled was bacon fryin' and coffee already perked. The shades in Mamma's room were drawn all the way down, but needles of sunshine slipped through a pin hole here and there. Outside I heard the crack of a bat in the road, Lizzy calling, "Strike one," and a man's voice in the kitchen wasn't Doctor Prout's.

I got up and tiptoed to see who it was. Mr. Charbonneau was sitting in my chair drinkin' a cup of coffee. Looked like he had just come in from playin' golf. I hurried upstairs to grab some clothes. Decided on a green-and-white striped seersucker jumper matched a green tee-shirt and my white sandals. The jumper pretty much covered the prickly dots on my knees.

"At last, you're up," Mamma called up from the hall. "Come have some breakfast. I've got your favorite French toast."

I came down and went into the bathroom to clean up. Took four times through with the big-bristle brush to get through my hair.

"Be right there," I yelled through the door.

Where was Tad? Why hadn't Mamma waked me for church?

"Home run!" Lizzy hollered.

Harper barked.

Time I came through the kitchen door, Mamma was putting a plate of French toast in front of Mr. Charbonneau.

"Good morning, young lady," he said. "No wonder Tad likes to visit so much," he pointed to his breakfast. "I hope you'll be joining your mother and me?"

I was about to go get my plate from the counter, but Mamma motioned for me to sit at her usual place at the table and said, "Your breakfast, Miss."

I felt like company. The French toast was the way she always served it on my birthday, with cinnamon and powdered sugar both.

Mamma sat down, but didn't make any for herself. She was wearin' her shift with the little boats, her pretty pink flats, and I could smell her hair just washed and fluffed dry. She had lipstick on, too, like she was ready to be going somewhere.

"Please, Stan," she motioned for Mr. Charbonneau to eat.

Glass crashed across the street.

"Billy, I told you to go play in the park!" Mrs. Carroll yelled.

Mr. Charbonneau laughed.

"Maybe Billy will be needing my services," he said.

I bit into the French toast I'd smothered with honey.

"Delicious," I said.

Mamma took a sip of her coffee, then put the mug down and looked at Mr. Charbonneau. Seemed like she already knew what he was going to say. I didn't know whether or not to be nervous.

162

"Orla, you may not know that I represent Mrs. Castleberry's interests. In other words, I'm her attorney."

He paused to take a bite of his breakfast. Mamma sipped her coffee again. I held a piece of French toast on my fork over my plate.

"Just after Easter, she came to see me to revise her will. Since you and your mother are beneficiaries..."

I put down my fork.

"Are what?" I asked.

Mamma smiled.

"Beneficiaries," Mr. Charbonneau said again, "persons who receive a gift or gifts from the deceased, from Mrs. Castleberry."

He took another bite.

"I wonder if you wouldn't mind coming with me and your mother to hear what Mrs. Castleberry has decided. I spoke with Doctor Prout this morning. He and Miss Yvette are putting Belle to rest in the family plot right now. We'll meet them up at the house at two o'clock."

I didn't know what to say, so I took another bite. Chewed. Swallowed. Mrs. Castleberry left us gifts. Maybe one of the statues. The honey tasted sweet and smooth. I looked at Mamma. She didn't smile, but she wasn't frowning, either.

Mr. Charbonneau wiped the powdered sugar off his mouth, folded his napkin on the table, and stood up.

"Well?" he said.

I licked the honey on my lips.

"Okay."

"I'll pick you ladies up just before two, then," he told Mamma.

She took his hand.

"Thank you, Stan," she said.

She had tears in her eyes. Mr. Charbonneau smiled at her and I saw Tad in his face.

Then he turned to me.

"Finish up, Orla. A person doesn't have this kind of breakfast every day. I'll tell Tad I saw you."

I nodded and finished eating while the two of them murmured in the hall. Felt like Mrs. Castleberry might be close by, somewhere she could see me. And she'd made sure Mr. Charbonneau delivered her message. I turned her ring round and round my finger with my thumb. Heard her voice in my mind. Legumes, it said perfectly.

Mr. Charbonneau drove away, gave two beeps as he went. Mamma stood at the door, waving.

When she came in, she said, "I'm going to read a little while."

She was holdin' up the newspaper Mr. Cowles flung from his car every morning, and I saw a photo of the Klan from yesterday on the front page.

"Let me see," I said.

"Me first," she answered.

I pretended to be angry, stamped my foot.

Mamma pointed to my dish.

"Finish your breakfast, young lady," she said, but she was grinning.

She started for the library room.

"No," I yelped and leapt out of my chair.

She stopped.

"Whatever is the matter with you?" she asked.

I had to tell the truth. The honey turned sour in my mouth. I felt wobbly with fear.

"Mamma," I said, and came around the table and into the hall.

She looked into my face.

"Yes?"

I pushed her aside, went by her into the room. It was completely clean. The coffee table was bare. Like nothing had ever been disturbed.

I turned back to her, quivering.

"I'm sorry, Mamma," I said. "I'm very sor—"

I couldn't finish. My hair fell about my face as I stared at the floor. Everything else in the room had belonged to somebody else. I had destroyed the only thing that was hers.

I sat on the floor in a heap, my head in my hands. I was no different than Mr. Cowles.

Mamma dropped the paper, knelt beside me, and pulled my head to her chest. She rubbed and rubbed my hair.

"No," she said, "I am, Orla. I truly am."

Chapter Twenty-Six

We all went into the dining room. Miss Yvette poured a glass of water at each place. Doctor Prout sat in Mrs. Castleberry's chair and Mr. Charbonneau faced him from the other end of the table. Mamma sat down next to me near the sideboard, and Miss Yvette looked across the table to the two of us, her back to the front windows.

"We finally managed to let her rest in peace," said Doctor Prout to no one in particular.

Miss Yvette nodded.

"The Klan must sleep late on Sundays," she said.

There was no mistaking the disgust in her voice. A vein stood out on her neck. She was still wearing a black dress, but her bangles were back on her wrists, jangling.

"Shall we begin?" said Mr. Charbonneau.

He smiled at Mamma like he had at our place. Then he put his briefcase on the table, opened it, and took out a leather binder with a tag that had Castleberry, Bellefleur Dubois typed on the front. He closed it and put it on the floor beside him.

He began to read.

"The house, its contents, the outbuildings, and the property go, of course, to you, Prout, as does the rest of your father's estate, passing from your mother to you. All bank accounts and stock holdings transfer automatically to your name."

Doctor Prout nodded and tapped his forefinger on the tablecloth.

"Yvette," Mr. Charbonneau faced her now, "your sister bequeaths you all furniture from your childhood home in France, as well as all her fine jewelry, with the exception of her engagement and wedding rings, which she leaves to Orla."

I heard my name, looked at Mr. Charbonneau, then to Mamma, and finally down at my hands. Doctor Prout cracked his knuckles. My face burned a little. Mamma rubbed my back. She didn't wear any rings, and now I had three. Mrs. Castleberry's engagement one was a square sapphire, with a white diamond either side. The wedding one was a circle of diamonds. I know because I cleaned both of them the last Friday of every month with the silver.

Miss Yvette strummed her bangles and winked at me like she had when I first explained my paintings to her. I hoped she wouldn't be angry. She'd have the child's chair with the painting of the bridge, Avignon, I remember Mrs. Castleberry saying. And the trundle bed with the secret drawer where Mrs. Castleberry kept her childhood toys. When I was little she had let me play with the wooden horses, les chevaux, while Mamma starched the whites.

Miss Yvette leaned over the table corner to Doctor Prout and murmured, "She's going to surprise you, *mon petit*."

Mamma looked at them fast, then studied her hands.

Doctor Prout took a sip of water. Miss Yvette stared across to Mamma, who had tucked down her head and folded her hands together on the table like she was in church.

"Here are some provisos," Mr. Charbonneau said.

Doctor Prout shifted in his chair. His brow was wet.

"While you own the house, et cetera, as I indicated earlier, Prout, your mother wishes Minerva and Orla to have life use, rent free."

Mamma shuddered, squeezed her hands tight, tried to stay still. But I could feel her shaking next to me. I wrapped my arm around hers. Doctor Prout bit his lips together.

"Suitable accommodations must remain available for both you and Yvette, however, should and/or when you visit."

"'Should,' Ha! My sister will never forgive me for belittling the South," said Miss Yvette.

You could tell from her voice, though, she wasn't angry.

Doctor Prout looked up and studied the chandelier, stopped tapping, then pushed himself out from the table a little, and tried to get Mamma to meet his eyes. But she didn't move.

"In addition, Orla's tuition at the Ursuline Academy in New Orleans will be covered, as long as she is found academically fit for the program."

Mamma's hands flew to her mouth and she didn't try not to cry anymore.

"Mamma!" I cried, and clapped my hands.

"Good for you, Belle," Miss Yvette whispered.

I'd get to go to a good school, like Tad. Wear a uniform had white gloves, meet some girls from places besides St. Suplice.

Mr. Charbonneau grinned at me, then continued.

168

"She may take private art classes weekly. Should her talent be enough, I entrust my sister Yvette to find her a suitable college or university where Orla might take an advanced degree. She may study in the United States, France, or Italy, or a combination thereof."

Mamma's fingers dug into my arm. I got hot inside my chest. My heart felt on fire. Bursts of surprises kept coming from Mrs. Castleberry. Things I never imagined could happen.

Doctor Prout said, "Minerva," and Mamma lifted her face.

They stared at one another over the table. Their faces told me nothing. Seemed they had a secret language didn't need words.

Mr. Charbonneau stopped talking, watched them watching each other. Miss Yvette's lips quivered. I waited, puzzled. Everybody seemed glad, but shaky, too.

Then, all of a sudden, Mamma was weeping out loud. But I knew she wasn't sad. I knew she was realizing I'd be an artist instead of a maid. When I realized it, too, I didn't feel like cryin' at all. My legs pumped back and forth under the table. My heart beat strong, the drum leadin' a parade. When I got famous enough, sold some pictures, I'd make sure Mamma wouldn't have to work at all.

Doctor Prout was smiling wide now. Smiling right at me.

He stood up, went over to Mamma, and gave her his handkerchief. She took it and he handed her her glass. She took a sip of water, then wiped her eyes and twisted the handkerchief in her hands. Doctor Prout went back to his chair. They still didn't talk, but he kept his eyes on her.

Mr. Charbonneau cleared his throat some, then stopped and took a drink of water, too.

"Minerva," he said.

169

Mamma looked at him, her face a question. She seemed in a daze.

"In 1961, Belle founded a mail-order company she calls French Lace. In secret, every Thursday evening, she taught nearly each of the women in Reverend Makepeace's congregation to make lace gloves, collars, and such, so they could earn money while caring for their own children at home."

I remembered the gloves on Mrs. Makepeace and the other Negro ladies at Mrs. Castleberry's funeral Mass.

"Belle names you president of the company upon her death. I'll meet with you during the week in my office to go over the particulars. You will take a salary for yourself and a portion of the company's gross income shall be used to provide scholarships for Negro children to St. Marguerite School."

Mamma was speechless. Her face had lost all its color.

"And she instructed me to give you this."

He handed Mamma one of Mrs. Castleberry's note cards with her initials on the front.

I leaned over to read what it said.

> *Minerva—*
> *Too late I have learned that you and I share the same stubborn determination regarding our children. Please forgive me the cost to them and to you.*
> *B.*

Mamma shook her head, sniffled and pulled me to her. She handed the note to Doctor Prout.

"What does she mean?" I asked

"Later," she whispered into my hair.

Doctor Prout read, then closed his mouth tight to keep the sound inside that was coming from deep in his chest.

Miss Yvette wiped a tear from her cheek and Mr. Charbonneau pushed back his chair.

"We can handle the rest at my office at your leisure," he said. "I'm sure you'll all have some questions. Just give a call and we'll arrange everything properly."

He faced Doctor Prout, "And you and I will bring Mr. Patrick his check ourselves, Prout?"

"Yes, thank you, Stan," said Doctor Prout, and he stood up.

Mr. Charbonneau reached for his briefcase.

"Oh," he remembered, "one more thing. Your mother was set on the Italians visiting, no matter what, Prout," he said.

Mamma and I looked at each other right away. She motioned me not to say a word.

Doctor Prout saw us, I could tell because his eyelids flickered before he turned to Mr. Charbonneau.

"We'll send a telegram tomorrow, then, tell them about my mother's passing, and invite them just the same," he said.

He ran his fingers through his hair and wiped the perspiration on his forehead off with his hand.

"Tante Yvette, you'll help me with the language?" he asked

Miss Yvette said, "*Si, non è problemo.*"

Doctor Prout seemed to have lost the words he was looking for.

Finally he said, "May I offer you anything, Stan?"

"Thanks, but no, Prout. The family's expecting me. We're going to celebrate my wife's birthday down at Sam's place with her family later."

"Please extend our greetings," Doctor Prout said.

Mr. Charbonneau collected all the papers, put them in his briefcase, hugged Mamma and me, kissed Miss Yvette's hand, and walked out to the veranda with Doctor Prout.

Miss Yvette came around the table to Mamma who was still sitting, twisting Doctor Prout's handkerchief in her hands.

"Don't think too much," she said, patting Mamma on the arm. "It will make your head hurt."

She and Mamma looked at each other like they understood something big.

Then Miss Yvette said to me, "Orla, my bedroom has the best light for painting. You might want to consider it for your studio. Plus it has its own bathroom."

Her eyes twinkled, and I realized for the first time they were the same blue as Mrs. Castleberry's.

I didn't know what to say except "Thank you," then I turned around in one slow circle and looked at the dining room like I'd never seen it before. The Chinese wallpaper with its turquoise sky and herons standing on one leg, the chair rail that matched the mahogany table, and the silk carpet mostly greens and ivory with its fringe all going in the same direction like Mrs. Castleberry insisted. Counted the eight dishes I'd dried so many times resting one inch apart across the mirrored china cabinet. The candlesticks I polished. Nothing looked different, but everything was. Just because she had said so. Even though she was dead.

"Excuse me, please," I said, and walked into the foyer towards the stairs. I felt like I was floating.

Mr. Charbonneau and Doctor Prout were standing on the veranda. Mr. Charbonneau held a long envelope in his hand.

"Your mother wanted me to give you this privately," he said.

He handed Doctor Prout the envelope.

"What..." Doctor Prout said.

I pretended to look for something in the telephone table drawer.

"Prout," he said, "she shared the contents with me. Let me know if I can be of any assistance."

They shook hands, and Doctor Prout walked down the steps with Mr. Charbonneau. I turned and watched them go to his car.

Miss Yvette and Mamma whispered in the dining room. Hard as I listened, I couldn't make out a word.

I tiptoed onto the veranda and stood behind one of the columns. I watched Doctor Prout stand by the bird bath and read. First he held the letter with two hands, then, after a while, he brought one hand up to his face and rubbed it around his mouth and his cheeks. He put the letter back into the envelope, walked around the bird bath a few times in a circle got bigger each time. Then he opened the letter again. A car passed by. He read some more. I could see his lips moving with the words. Finally he folded the letter again, put it into the envelope, stuck it into his shirt pocket so it stood up like a tower, skimmed his hands over the water in the bird bath, and started back to the veranda.

"Mother," I heard him say, as I held the screen so it wouldn't slam behind me.

I walked to the stairs. Mamma came out the dining room and followed me to the railing. She looked like she had a fever, or at least a very bad cold. Still had Doctor Prout's handkerchief in her hand, wet and wrinkled now.

"Did you know, Mamma, did she tell you?"

Mamma held me in her arms.

"No, Orla, it's been a surprise. If Mr. Charbonneau hadn't stopped by this morning to prepare me, I'd have had a heart attack myself."

173

I pushed her away and started up the stairs.

"Where are you going?" Mamma asked.

It seemed I didn't have a choice.

"The attic," I said.

Mamma stood quiet a moment, then said, "I think I'll write Archbishop Rummel. He ought to know."

I could hear him in my mind, "Remember, Minerva, all will be well."

"Mamma," I said, and looked at her like she'd lost her mind.

She sat down on the chair by the telephone and looked up at me through the railing.

"What?" she said.

"He already did, Mamma. That's what he was telling you yesterday. He already did."

Mamma's face turned into something shining and she smiled. Then Doctor Prout walked in. He looked like a ghost. Didn't say a word, just opened the door to his daddy's library, went in and closed the door behind him.

Chapter Twenty-Seven

The stairs felt narrow and high, a longer walk than before. But everything was just the way we left it when Mrs. Castleberry had her attack. I wasn't afraid, just missing her. I found Baby Jesus, slid his box between Mary and Joseph, propped up Gabriel against the wood and straw manger, then stretched myself down on the floor beside them.

"Thank you," I said, hopin' someone could hear.

It was quiet and musty and not-quite-bright. Baby Jesus' lips were still red, though, and Mary looked calm. I knew they weren't real, just statues, but maybe the real ones heard. Maybe Mrs. Castleberry was with them now. I hoped the angels had brought her to Paradise, that Paradise really existed.

I'd miss our little house, especially the sleeping porch and hearin' Mamma in the kitchen every morning, but then I thought of all the times I'd spent here, too. More than at home. Every Easter Sunday I could remember. Most every Monday, when Mamma'd deliver the mending. Christmas, when Mrs. Castleberry gave Mamma a dozen books and me little pretend drums filled with cinnamon sticks and homemade molasses lollipops. Every summer for French lessons around the picnic table, "so we can show my sister Yvette we are not as backward as she thinks in St. Suplice."

We had just started getting ready for the Italians. Weren't nearly done. Mrs. Castleberry had lots more to teach me about gesso and opera, Fiesole, and the war. She lent me her records and had Mr. Patrick bring down her easel. She was turnin' Tad into a real historian and makin' having Negroes over for lunch as common as iced tea.

"Why'd she have to die?" I asked out loud.

None of the statues answered.

Dawned on me that all the dead people I know of still feel alive. My Daddy, Old Doctor Castleberry, now Mrs. Castleberry. All of them gone and leaving me reminders they were here once, breathing same as I was now. My Daddy built nearly every shelf in our house, my old crib and the sleepin' porch bed. Old Doctor Castleberry left a whole library and hundreds of babies he helped get born.

Now, even before I'd had much time to think it over, I knew Mrs. Castleberry had left me the most. She and I had spent practically my whole life together. If it hadn't been for her, I'd never have met Miss Yvette and been chosen a "promising young artist of America." Never heard opera, or be getting ready to meet Italians, never sat at the big mahogany table in the formal dining room, seen a White lady sit down to lunch with Reverend Makepeace. I wouldn't have thought of Mamma with a chignon or be meeting Doctor Prout, learned the difference between "assayer" and "essayer," milk and clotted cream.

I thought of her now. Seemed she must be somewhere near the stars, back of a pleasant field where some ponies and maybe a few sheep were grazing. There'd be other people, too. People like her who wanted things nice and right at the same time. No nonsense and plenty of chances. Good manners and carefulness. Hard work and lots of fresh-squeezed lemonade to drink. Scary sometimes, once in a while even mean. But mostly good, especially when a body didn't know her plans.

I strained to see her. She was sitting in a high-backed wicker chair, her legs crossed at her ankles, "the way ladies sit, Orla," wearing one of her dresses with little flowers, hair drawn back, but not too tight, "lest one look severe, Minerva," reaching out her hand to someone new, just arriving.

"Good evening, Orla Gwen, and isn't it a lovely evening? Let me show you this interesting picture of Giverny...."

I most felt crazy, thinking she was speaking, hearing her voice the way I hear the opera in my mind. I wanted to tell her, to take her hand in mine.

"Evening, Mrs. Castleberry. Not a cloud in the sky. Thank you for showing me things. Thank you for helping me paint. I sure will miss seeing you."

All of a sudden, loneliness washed over me and I reached for Baby Jesus. But he was only glass, so I covered my eyes with my hands and tried to memorize her face, to draw her permanently in my mind. Her blue eyes looked right at me and she sat up straight, her legs together and tilted a little to the side. She'd be about to smile, but not yet. Not until I answered, "Here I am, Mrs. Castleberry." Then she'd open her arms.

Don't know how long I was asleep. It was still daytime when I opened my eyes, but the sun shone in the small windows at an angle. Someone yanked the door below and scraped up the stairs. I felt stiff, rubbed by eyes, blinked so I could see better. Doctor Prout stood over me. I felt embarrassed, his seein' me laying down in an attic and all. But he acted like there was nothing unusual going on.

"Minerva told me I'd find you here. I understand you helped my mother when she took ill showing you the statues. Thank you, Orla. Thank you for helping her."

He stooped down a bit and offered both his hands. I reached for them and he pulled me up.

"Thanks," I said, and smoothed my jumper.

I stood up straight. Doctor Prout looked around the attic. He rubbed his hand on Mary's head.

"We always had them on the veranda at Christmas," he said, mostly to himself.

I wondered where Doctor Prout spent Christmas. He hadn't come home any of the times I was here.

Then to me, "They came from Italy."

I nodded, stood by the wood manger. "Yes, Mrs. Castleberry told me the whole story, how they're made, that Egidio taught the children."

I slid my hand down Mary's blue cloak. Doctor Prout looked distracted.

"My father visited there twice a year. He went to see his orphans. 'My orphans,' he called them."

He looked back at me. His mouth drooped on either side. Appeared like all the breath had been taken out of him.

"I used to wonder why my mother never went with him."

I didn't know if I was supposed to say, "Why didn't she?" or "Is that so?" so I didn't say anything, just stood and waited.

Then Doctor Prout stooped down like a baseball catcher and faced me.

"I'm sorry you had to see her take ill. Your mother told me you went for some water, that you kept her calm."

My face burned and my eyes began to water.

"But she died," I said. "I let her die."

I felt as broken as Gabriel.

Doctor Prout put his big hands on my shoulders.

"Don't ever think that, Orla," he said, his voice low, but sounding sure.

I looked at him.

"It was for you that she lived," he said. "I realize that now."

He tried to smile, then straightened up and turned toward the stairs.

"Come on," he said, reaching out his hands again to mine.

I looked at the family of statues behind me, then turned away from them and followed Doctor Prout downstairs, him first, me behind, our fingers touching. Somehow it felt right we should walk through the narrow stairway together.

Downstairs in the foyer, we had to blink because of the sun. It was quiet except for the banner fluttering outside.

"What do you say we take a ride?" Doctor Prout said, like he'd just woke up again.

I didn't know if I wanted to be alone with him.

"I could use a cup of Sam's peach ice cream on a Sunday afternoon."

"Where's Mamma?" I asked.

He picked up his car keys off the telephone table.

"Tante Yvette is showing her the lace catalogue. They won't even notice we're gone."

I didn't know what to say.

"Here," Doctor Prout said, pulling his little notebook out of his breast pocket. "We'll write them."

He took his pen top off with his mouth, then printed on the little page: *Gone for ice cream, O and P.*

He put it on the bottom step, where Mamma or Miss Yvette would be sure to see it. I heard Mamma's voice upstairs. Miss Yvette said something made Mamma laugh out loud.

"Maybe I should..." I said, turning to go up to them.

"Come on," Doctor Prout grabbed my hand, "I'll show you where your mother and I used to hide when we were supposed to be at clubs after school."

I wanted to hate him for tryin' to steal my Mamma. But he kept bein' nice to me, kinda like Mrs. Castleberry, only not strict. His voice felt like a comfortable room.

"Okay," I said, but I still wasn't sure.

He held the door of the station wagon open for me to get in. Then we backed out the drive. I looked up at the house. His, and now mine and Mamma's, too. I glanced over to Doctor Prout, who was humming something not really music, but more like a couple of notes repeating. I felt nervous, but a little excited, too.

"Did you ever get caught?" I asked.

Doctor Prout turned to me as we started toward the Haldecott's place.

"You bet."

Then he smiled. His teeth were very straight.

He got quiet again, then all of a sudden threw back his head and laughed out loud, "You bet we did, but not for a very long time."

He laughed again, happy, like he was remembering. I bet he was thinking of seein' Mamma naked. Hearin' her moan when he kissed her. I hated him again, moved close to the door as I could, wrapped my fingers around the handle. So many questions I wanted to ask him. But instead I stared ahead while he drove me to only God knew where.

Chapter Twenty-Eight

We sped right by the Haldecott's, way down to Hester's Ridge, and across the river by the railroad tracks on a one-way road. Doctor Prout didn't drive like Mr. Patrick.

"Almost there," he said.

I sat up close to the windshield to see ahead.

"What we used to do all through high school was to swim from the Haldecott's dock all the way across the river, then clamber right to there."

We got out of the car and I could see an abandoned boathouse below us and a dock farther down the glade. The ground was thick with vines and fallen branches. A path snaked toward the water from underneath the awning of trees.

"We used to signal each other with one of the Haldecott's tarps," Doctor Prout said. He chuckled out loud. "Actually, we stole it, Orla. But I don't think Mrs. Haldecott ever knew."

I looked up at him in surprise. No grownup ever told me something bad they did on purpose before.

"We'd drape it over the chair to mean, 'Meet me,' and store it in the boat house otherwise."

I already knew Mamma lied to me, but I had never thought about her lyin' to her parents before. She had a whole life I didn't know one thing about until I started sneaking around and lying, too.

"We smoked cigarettes we weren't supposed to and one time, just before graduation, we got ourselves a bottle of champagne from my father's liquor cabinet and had ourselves a good-bye party."

I couldn't believe he was telling me. Only time I saw Mamma drink was at midnight on New Year's Eve or at the fair and the Fourth of July picnic. Now I imagined her in her bathing suit with a glass in her hand and coughing from the smoke like Billy Carroll did behind Sam's Fish Shack.

We about slid down to the boathouse—the roof was all squished in with some big branches over it, and I could see a dirty blue tarp was still in there.

"Who else came?" I asked.

Doctor Prout was walking down toward the dock, but turned back to me.

"Why, nobody." He seemed surprised I'd asked. "Just your mother and me. My parents were sending me off to Europe for the summer as a graduation present and then directly to college up North in September."

He hurried ahead. I tried to keep up with him, watching for snakes.

"And Mamma was just about to get married, right?"

I flushed at my question, but it burst right out of me.

"Yes," he said.

He drew out the word so it sounded like a hiss in the afternoon air.

Doctor Prout stopped walking and looked right at me.

"Much to my dismay, I might add."

He put his hands together and cracked his fingers three times.

"Perhaps she's told you herself, I wanted her to marry me."

He ran his fingers through his hair. I nodded yes.

"We wanted to marry each other."

He said it like it was a math fact.

"Ouch!"

I had stepped on something pointy. My toe was bleeding.

"Are you okay?" he asked.

I sat down on the ground, took off my sandal, and turned my foot over in my hand. Spit a few times on the blood, then wiped it with my fingers. Doctor Prout laughed, but not like he thought I was silly. More like he was enjoying himself.

He knelt and motioned for my foot. I stuck out my leg and he studied it. I looked up and watched his face.

"You will survive," he said, serious-like, then laughed again.

"Why didn't you? Marry her, I mean."

He stopped, pulled some weedy thing out the ground and, picking one shoot off at a time, aimed it like an arrow at a tree leaned toward the river.

When he was done he sat down,too, across from me. "It sounds ridiculous to say so now; I cannot believe it myself, but Mother wouldn't let me. Even when Father lobbied on my behalf."

He looked dumbfounded.

"My father, you know, loved your mother. 'A girl with spirit,' he would say whenever her name was mentioned."

Talking to him most didn't feel like talking to a grownup at all. Might have been Tad and me, he acted so comfortable.

Even the big spider that dropped onto his head he just brushed off, saying, "Hmmm, you are a dandy."

We got up again and walked onto the dock. I liked how I could feel the river rushing under me making me rock and sway. Doctor Prout sat down, took off his shoes and socks, rolled up his pants, and stuck his feet in the water.

"Your mother," he said. "Your mother was the prettiest and smartest girl at school."

He splashed his feet up and down.

"Join me?" he asked.

I sat down, but not too close. I thought of Mamma's bathing suit and the writing inside the bra. I looked over at his hands that felt so good on my shoulders, knew they'd touched Mamma's breasts, probably lots of times, just yesterday, even. I wanted to forget that, but I couldn't. I was hot with shame. I wanted to slap him.

I moved farther toward my edge of the dock and put my sandals behind me. My feet just skimmed the water. We sat for a long time. I kept tryin' to think of something regular that didn't make my stomach all fluttery, like crackers or toothpaste. But our faces bobbed next to each other in the water with a wavy space in between, where every now and then other faces appeared. First my Daddy's, then Mamma's, and Mrs. Castleberry's, too. They all danced in the water, coming and going, all of them trying to tell me something I should know.

"Look!" Doctor Prout shouted.

I followed his finger. Out mid-river, three flying fish leapt out of the water, made a rainbow arc, then dove back into the rush.

They were beautiful. Graceful. Full of grace.

Doctor Prout turned to me.

"Up North, you know, people go out on large ferries off the Cape and wait for whales."

The fish jumped again. I'd make my brush copy them later.

"When my father used to take me fishing, I preferred watching the life on the river to the fishing itself."

Doctor Prout splashed some water on his hands.

"But Father thought fishing taught patience. I guess he believed I needed some."

He got quiet again. I looked at our toes, tryin' to make myself believe they didn't match.

"What was your daddy like?" I asked.

I knew it wasn't fair for me to ask, since I already knew something about Old Doctor Castleberry that he had just found out. But it seemed to me that even when a body did know something, that something still had another surprise waiting right next to it anyway. The way a branch turns out to be a snake, or the very nicest clerk in the grocery is a member of the Klan. I guess the surprises worked the other way, too, sometimes. Like Mrs. Castleberry bein' really generous to Mamma in her will. Or me getting to paint for real my whole life.

"Well, for one thing, he had bushy red hair. It was the first characteristic about him people noticed. And he loved being a doctor. He just loved his patients."

Doctor Prout got real quiet. He looked down into the water. A motor boat sped by, distracting him, and he waved. He kicked his feet like scissors in the water.

"Saturdays he took me on rounds with him all around St. Suplice, and some of the neighboring parishes, as well."

I swatted the mosquitoes away.

"What's 'rounds'?" I asked.

Doctor Prout cracked his hands again.

"They are a doctor's visitations to his patients."

I took my feet up out of the water, turned to Doctor Prout, and held my arms around my knees.

"Did you want to go?" I asked.

Doctor Prout chuckled again.

"You bet. Mostly to get away from Mother for a while, I am slightly embarrassed to tell you."

Another secret.

"Why?"

He splashed his face with water.

"She was usually set on improving me in some fashion—correcting my posture, having me practice ballroom dancing, wanting me to phone stuffy Maryellen Carville, whose parents were friends of hers at The Links."

I thought about how Mrs. Castleberry was always telling me to act like a lady. How she bossed Father Carriere around. How she made Mamma and Mr. Patrick get so tired.

"Father, on the other hand, ..."

He stopped, looked at my face, carefully, slowly.

"Are you sure this is interesting to you?" he asked.

I wiggled my toes in the wet.

"Keep going," I said, then remembered, "please."

"Well, then," he said, "Father and Mother had different mindsets. They were a fine couple, you understand, but had contrary outlooks about people."

The boat sped by the other direction. We both waved.

"Mother found St. Suplice stifling. That is why she insisted I go away, to Europe, Boston, New York."

She must have thought I should go, too.

Doctor Prout continued.

"However, she was good to the town. She bought books for the library, saw to it that the church had altar linens and the like."

I remembered her pointing out the vestments Father Carriere wore. Mamma's pile of books every Christmas.

The train whistle sounded in the distance. Soon the five o'clock would pass through Hester's Ridge.

"People appreciated her, they understood she was a perfectionist, a well-intentioned one. But they loved Father. They opened up to him, felt he was a kindred spirit."

Doctor Prout rubbed water on both his arms.

"To Father, people were not just projects needing improvement; they were folks he sewed up some when they ripped."

I thought of a big red-headed man holding a needle and thread, kinda like a good giant in a fairy tale.

Doctor Prout rubbed his hands over his face.

"Mother always told him, 'Comb your hair, Arthur.'"

I felt my hair mussing in the breeze. Doctor Prout smiled.

"But he never did, except for once in the morning just out of the shower."

Doctor Prout patted his own hair in imitation.

"'How would anyone know me, Belle?' he would say, always leaning down to kiss Mother's forehead."

I tried to imagine Mrs. Castleberry kissing him back.

"What did she say?" I asked.

Doctor Prout considered. He stood up on the dock, rolled down his pant legs, listened to the train whistle getting closer and closer.

"Her responses varied," he said.

He turned and started up toward the car. I picked up my sandals and followed him.

"One time she..."

But the train screamed through Hester's Ridge above us so I couldn't hear a word.

Chapter Twenty-Nine

Mrs. Charbonneau was just blowin' out her birthday candles when we got to Sam's. We clapped with all the other customers, then waited in line to order two pints of homemade ice cream, one peach, the other strawberry. Doctor Prout told Sam he often walked to Fenway Park from work to see the Boston Red Sox play, and I took Tad aside to tell him about Doctor Prout and Mamma stealin' the champagne. It was nearly suppertime, and we had to get the ice cream back before it melted.

"Oh, good, you're here," Miss Yvette said, looking up from one of the chaise lounges on the veranda.

Mamma sat next to her. They were both drinking something clear out of tall glasses with limes in them.

"I'll put this in the freezer," I said, taking the ice cream from Doctor Prout.

Mamma stood up and looked at the two of us.

"Where on earth have you been all this time?" she asked.

I looked at Doctor Prout. He put his fingers to his lips. I smiled.

"Orla and I will get supper," he said.

Mamma put her hand to her chest, like she had been shot. Miss Yvette sat up straighter on the chaise lounge.

"You will?" she said.

"How do you think I have survived the North all these years?" he asked.

Miss Yvette snapped, "The same way I have, *mon petit*, restaurants and the generosity of curious strangers."

Doctor Prout's head dropped forward. He made a pretending-to-be-hurt face.

"Come on," he said, "let's leave these harpies out here."

He didn't know where anything was. I found the leftover ham in the refrigerator.

"How about an omelet?" I suggested.

Doctor Prout washed his hands. I opened the vegetable bin and pulled out a red pepper and some scallions. There was a small wedge of cheese above, too. I got Mrs. Castleberry's biggest iron frying pan, cut a piece of butter for it, then let the butter melt on the stove.

I cracked eight eggs into a bowl and said, "Will you beat them?" to Doctor Prout.

When he was done, I handed him the knife for the vegetables.

I set the dining room simply, not with the monogrammed silver, just with the everyday set Mrs. Castleberry used when she ate alone.

"What else?" Doctor Prout asked.

I looked in the bread drawer.

"How about some rolls?"

He took them from me. I got onto the stool and opened the cabinet where we kept the bread baskets.

"Good," he said.

Then he started rummaging around the other cabinets.

"Aha, at last," he said.

I looked at the jar in his hands. It was the crab apples Mrs. Castleberry candied herself every year. He twisted the top off with a pop and we put the apples in a white dish I picked so their color'd show best.

Doctor Prout sat at the kitchen table watching me mix the vegetables into the egg bowl.

When I lit the oven and put the whole iron fryin' pan in, he said, "Now this is new to me."

I closed the over door.

"Mrs. Castleberry showed me how to make a baked omelet," I said. "She read about them in one of the orphanage newsletters. Italian eggs."

Doctor Prout stood up.

"When will it be ready?" he asked.

I looked at the clock.

"Twenty minutes."

"Good," he said, "we can join the ladies. Would you care for a Shirley Temple?" he asked.

I looked at him, confused. I had seen some movies with her in them.

"Go," he said. "Arrange yourself on the veranda. And do not let them amuse themselves by criticizing me."

I felt like we were playing house, the way kids do in the lower grades, with pretend fruit made of wood and stoves small enough for five-year-old hands to reach. The little boys would drive their trucks, zoom zoom, into the kindergarten kitchen, and the little girls would set the table with bright red plastic dishes.

I looked at the clock again, set the timer on the stove, and went outside. I pulled a second chaise lounge closer to Mamma and lay myself across it like Miss Yvette. In a little

190

while, Doctor Prout brought me a strawberry-colored drink with a cherry in it tasted like ginger ale and something else.

I looked at it.

"Well, now," Mamma said.

"Grenadine, dear, that's what makes it red," Miss Yvette said.

Doctor Prout had a beer mug in his hand. I felt like I was starring in a Hollywood movie.

"To Belle," said Miss Yvette.

She raised her glass.

"Mother," said Doctor Prout, holding his glass up, too.

Mamma looked at me, but instead of raising her glass, too, she just put her drink to her lips, sipped once, then again.

I tasted mine, just a little at first, then a big gulp. I hadn't even known I was thirsty.

Nobody spoke. The air hung wet and thick around us. A bee hovered over one of the big flower urns, its black and yellow stripes makin' me think of tigers. A brown beetle made its way from underneath the urn across the top step of the veranda and disappeared into a space in the wood. My fingers moistened around the glass as the ice in my drink melted. We were separate, one from the other, each alone in our thoughts. I half-expected Mrs. Castleberry to jump out from behind one of the chairs and yell, "Boo!"

Then, like a signal had been given, we all put our glasses to our mouths together. Reminded me of an orchestra needing to keep the same time. Only we hadn't practiced yet.

An animal screeched in the bushes by the garage. The sun glinted off the station wagon in the driveway. The potting shed door was closed and no birds splashed in the bird bath. The Castleberry veranda wasn't full, but it wasn't empty, either. The strange thing was, the person who'd gotten us all here was gone for good. We'd have to decide the rest for ourselves. I felt sad, happy, excited, and afraid all at once.

Miss Yvette would go back to New York, of course. And I guess Mamma and me would learn to call the Castleberry place home. About Doctor Prout, I couldn't tell. Wasn't sure. He'd been away a long time. But maybe it wasn't just Mamma he wanted. This afternoon it seemed like he wanted me, too.

The timer buzzed. I put down my drink and stood. Doctor Prout got up, too, finished his beer in two gulps, and reached out his hand. He opened the screen door, then stood aside to let me go in ahead of him. I felt like the lady Mrs. Castleberry had wanted me to become.

"Thank you," I said.

Doctor Prout and I walked into the kitchen together. He put on the oven mitts and pulled the omelet out of the oven. I brought the rolls and the candied apples to the dining room table. He followed and the puffed eggs settled nicely, steam rising out of the iron pan.

"Dinner is served," he bellowed onto the veranda.

Then he pulled out Mrs. Castleberry's chair and motioned for me to sit down. He pushed my chair close to the table and kissed the top of my head, hardly upsetting my curls. As she came in, Mamma saw. Her face had been so rested this morning wrinkled before my eyes till it looked like how I'd felt when I heard her moaning in his arms the day before.

Chapter Thirty

Doctor Prout drove us home on his way over to Mr. Patrick's. It was just dark.

Before we got out of the car, he said, "I wonder if I might stop by later, Minerva."

Mamma didn't even look at him.

"I'll leave the porch light on," is all she said.

We went inside before he drove off. The house felt small, hot, and still. Even so, it'd be hard to leave it for good. It wasn't grand like the Castleberry place, but it fit Mamma and me just right. Room enough for us to be alone reading or painting, a table for playing cards with Lizzy and her mamma, the porch for working outside with Tad.

After my bubble bath, I went upstairs, got out a sketch pad, and began drawing in charcoal. I wanted to fix each room on paper so I wouldn't forget. I felt clean and soft and ready. My striped pajamas smelled nice from the lilac paper in my drawer. But before I knew it, I had gotten out the watercolors to paint a flying fish.

My brush curved on the parchment. Yellow, green, blue, silver flecked the splash. Heat hung orange on the water, wavelets lapped gray at my feet. Doctor Prout's mouth dropped speckled words. Faces bobbed at me fish-mouthed, OrlaOrlaOrla. Then from the rush, the leap of something alive. Gift from the river. Graceful. Full of grace.

My mind was an island rising. Mamma might have run away, I wouldn't have cared. Heaviness was gone. No one felt dead. My hand moving the brush. Salvation.

"Orla," Mamma stood at the bottom of the stairs. "Answer me!"

I stuck my head out my bedroom door. Mamma'd pulled her hair up into a chignon and was wearin' open sandals that used to be Mrs. Haldecott's daughter's. Her blouse was sleeveless and she had the first three buttons open so you could see where her bra began. It was the lace. Her eyes were made up and her lipstick matched the polish on her toes.

"When Doctor Prout comes, I'm going to show him the Contessa's letter you discovered. Give us some privacy, okay?"

I didn't answer, just walked down a few steps and had her look at my painting still wet. A long fish crossed the paper mid-arch. Bubbles trailed on the water. In the background, Doctor Prout and me on the dock, and above it, the boat house falling apart.

"I want to hang it in my new room," I said.

Mamma studied the painting.

"That's where you went today," she said.

I leaned on the stair rail.

"He said you stole the tarp."

Mamma acted like she didn't hear.

"And drank champagne."

194

Mamma walked into the kitchen with me trailing behind. She reached up over the table and pulled the string that started the ceiling fan.

"Kiss me good-night now. I'll come up after he leaves," she said.

She put two glasses into the freezer to frost. Got the broom and swept under the table. Hummed.

I had been dismissed.

I heard Mrs. Castleberry's voice, "That will be all for today, Orla."

Mamma brushed the crumbs into the garbage pail. Rinsed the coffee cups left from breakfast.

I turned my back, held my painting like a tray, both hands under it, so the colors wouldn't run, and walked upstairs.

She didn't even say, "Hey, you, where's my kiss?" like she did every morning I'd ever left for school.

I put the painting on the floor to dry, then lay on my bed and stared at the ceiling. The stars and moon I'd cut out of butcher paper and dipped in finger paints, then taped up there had curled in the damp. Heaven wilting.

I heard Mamma open the pantry door and pull out some jars. She cracked ice from the freezer trays and dumped them into a bucket. "Oh, by the way, Prout, here's another note reminding you that you have a sister. Cheers."

Mrs. Carroll hollered, "Billy, time to come in," and Harper barked in reply.

The street lights came on and palm fronds scratched one another in the alley by Miss Cruz's place. I got up, turned on the hall light, sat down on the top step, and waited.

Doctor Prout's car slowed to a stop out front. When he knocked, I came downstairs and let him in. He was holding a bottle wrapped in silver paper and a long envelope said

Prout, upon my death, in Mrs. Castleberry's handwriting. It was the one he had opened out by the birdbath, the one with the letter must have told him he was not his daddy's only child. Mamma came out of the kitchen with a lime in her hand.

"Orla was just going up to bed," she said.

She pointed up the stairs. Her stare said she was serious, but I stuck my tongue out at her anyway. She glared. Doctor Prout tried not to laugh. Lines thin as spider legs crawled out the corners of both her eyes. I stared back. A car going too fast squealed by. My sleeves stuck to my armpits.

When I was sure she wouldn't start a fight in front of him, I took my time and turned away from her and, polite as I could, said, "Night," to Doctor Prout.

He watched us both.

I walked up the stairs like they were some wonderful tree to climb.

"I'll just slice the limes," Mamma said, and Doctor Prout followed her into the kitchen.

"Good night, Orla," he said, as I stroked the stair rail.

I stretched out on the floor, my feet reaching into the bedroom, my head just at the top of the stairs. I spread my hair out behind so strands of it hung over and down the first step. I blinked to get used to the dark. After a while I could see the cracks on the ceiling traveled across the molding and down onto the walls. My chest rose up and down, up and down. I breathed in time to the insects.

Doctor Prout and Mamma clinked their glasses together. Their voices talked slowly at first, then faster, but I couldn't make out the words. When I'd followed the longest crack right to the molding on the floor, they weren't talking at all. I took a breath deep enough to fill my chest with air, then turned on my side and put my ear to the floorboards to listen. Silence.

At last the chairs scraped and their feet shuffled. The icebox door opened and shut. Water ran out of the faucet, and the two of them made their way into the library room. They mustn't have noticed me, 'cause they went right by. Only sounds were the bugs and an owl hooting back of the house.

I stood up, stretched, and came down to the bathroom, made sure to make noise—opened the door so they'd hear the flush, washed my hands at the sink, then padded back upstairs. Only thing was, after I closed my bedroom door, click, I opened it again, softly, slowly, and crawled back down onto the stairway. The hall was dark except for the glow of the reading lamp in the library room. I heard Doctor Prout's voice.

"Do you think she knows?"

The owl hooted twice.

Then, long enough for the hall clock to tick seventeen times, "I don't think so," said Mamma.

Coasters clattered on the coffee table.

"He visited every October and every May," said Doctor Prout.

"Oh, you meant Gabriella. Of course."

Mamma sounded mean.

Doctor Prout got up, walked around the couch, the floor creaking every time he got to the loose slat. Circled and circled.

"Yes. Why, do you think...?"

Mr. Carroll whistled loud, then hollered, "Billy, I'm locking the door in five minutes."

Mamma sneezed.

"Bless you," he said.

"I guess you'll have to ask the Contessa."

Doctor Prout stood still and his glass clunked on the coffee table.

Mamma said, "Do you want more ice?"

"I'll get it."

He walked by the stairs to the kitchen, opened the icebox, filled his glass again, then went back to the library room.

"At least she knew him," Mamma said.

Her voice dropped a boulder into the room.

The lamp crashed to the floor.

"Damn!" he said.

Light streamed sideways into the hallway. My shoulders tightened. I tensed my ears, held my breath.

"You'll wake her!" Mamma sounded alarmed.

Somebody put the lamp back.

"It's not broken," Doctor Prout said.

Mamma strode outside onto the porch. He followed behind. I couldn't hear them at all.

I thought a minute, then crawled from the top of the stairs to the front of the house and knelt by the dormers over the porch. One of the windows always fell loose, so I had a couple of inches of screen. Back and forth, back and forth, the rocker tested the floor. Mamma's voice rose and dipped.

"You think you can just come back now that your mother is dead, make friends, show her a good time, tell her what a bad girl I was?"

The rocker stopped.

"Do you even know her birthday?" Mamma asked.

I grabbed the edge of my Daddy's robe and twisted it in my hands. She was supposed to be talking to him about Gabriella.

"Minerva," he said, pleading.

Mamma's whisper got louder.

"I'll take what I can," she said, her words like scissors cutting. "But not for her. I won't allow it. At least your father cared!"

Insect voices rose in a frenzy. I brought the edge of the robe to my mouth. The cry inside me struggled to get out, but I pushed the cotton in until it made me gag.

"Let go," she said.

"No," he answered.

My heart pounded and I pressed my face to the floor. Mamma was crying below, not loud or urgent, even. Just soft, lonely crying.

Rain began to fall, first big drops, one at a time, pinging the roof and the gables. Then fast and faster, till it was all I could hear.

I tiptoed back toward my room. When I got to the top of the stairs, I saw Doctor Prout hold the screen door for Mamma to come in. He followed her into the kitchen, but no lights came on. I waited and waited. The rain drummed and I heard it slide down the drain spouts outside. The owl had gone silent.

I tiptoed down the steps in the dark. My bare feet felt each tread. In the hallway, I pressed myself against the wall, inched toward the kitchen, my face turned toward the archway. I held the wall with my palms, tried to move with the rain, peered around the molding.

Doctor Prout's shadow was bent over the table and Mamma's legs were wrapped around him. He thrust and thrust, stabbing her.

I felt my knees go weak. Still I stared.

Rain dented the roof. Mamma reached up her arms. Doctor Prout flung himself onto her, and the table lurched.

I ran for the stairs, but not soon enough.

"More," Mamma gasped, before I could escape. "More, Prout, more."

I pounded the stairs, leapt onto my bed become a spinning raft. Dizzy, I clung to the mattress, flung myself over back to front, front to back. My legs would not be still. My scalp itched fire. My tongue roamed my teeth, and the alarm clock ticking told me yes, this is your life, it is true.

The rain kept on while I counted all the way up to a thousand and said twenty Glory Be's. But why should I pray? Whywhywhywhywhy?

Then, suddenly, like the world had ended all at once, there was nothing but silence. The rain had stopped, the insects grown too swollen to speak, the owl fled into a tree. I breathed again, waiting.

The front door closed. Doctor Prout's car rumbled away. I sat on the edge of my bed and looked into the black hall. Mamma tiptoed up the stairs. Bent to switch on the night light in the upstairs hall. She stood in my bedroom doorway, then jumped when she saw me awake.

She studied me, waited for a hint. But I sat with my hands underneath me, my legs slack and dangling. Felt my solitary breath. Exhaled.

"I've come to tuck you in," she said, her voice maple syrup. "Like I promised."

I wanted her to, I wanted her to smooth my hair, to tell me how her mamma had made curtains out of string, to hold my fingers, this is the church, this is the steeple, open the doors, here all the people. I wanted us to be two again, walking into town in matching dresses she had sewn, they look brand new, you'd never know they were somebody else's. I wanted her the way I used to think she was, straight and pretty, honest and mine. I really wanted that.

Instead, I slid off the bed, walked the tightrope barefoot towards her, and, certain as the night, closed the door against her face.

"Go away," I said. "Just go away."

My voice was a plank.

She didn't move.

My toes gripped the floor. I stared at the wood between us. I grasped the doorknob in my hand, deciding. Then, the way a body lets go the safety line when her arms give out, I dropped my hand to my side. I turned from the door and walked back to the bed. I lay myself down and faced the night. When the mattress springs quieted from my settling, Mamma walked slowly down the stairs. Saddest part was I only felt relief.

Chapter Thirty-One

"Sam, Sam! There's a nigger lady in the bathroom!"

Katie Cowles stood screaming under the Whites Only sign, pointing at the bathroom said Femmes over the mermaid decal. She looked even smaller than usual. Nobody'd have thought she was already seven.

Tad and I had been eating red hots with Mr. Patrick at Sam's Fish Shack. Weren't for Mr. Patrick, I might'a stayed in my room all day. But he beeped the horn till I knew Mamma'd already gone, so I went down to the car.

"Mrs. Castleberry finally treated me White, Orla. She left me enough money so that now I'm practically a rich man. All I got to do is mow her lawn if I want to," he told me.

We drove over to Tad's house. Mamma'd already phoned ahead. Tad was to come to the Castleberry place later to look at more war papers Doctor Prout thought he should see.

Soon as we got to Sam's place, Mr. Patrick called out, "Lunch for all the kids, Sam."

He put a twenty-dollar bill onto the counter. Waiting, he held his cane crosswise between his hands like a soft-shoe dancer.

Soon Tad, then Katie Cowles and Billy Carroll, who had been playing on the swings and slide, Mr. Patrick, Sam, and I were feasting on hot dogs, fries, clam rolls, and ice cream. Father Carriere stopped by to pick up some clam broth, and Mrs. Allaire struggled out her son's car to put in an order of stuffed shrimp for a crowd next Friday. As usual, Sam's radio was crackling, made it annoying to listen.

"To Mrs. Castleberry!" Mr. Patrick said, raising his beer. "Never thought I'd hear myself say that!" Sam laughed out loud as he went back inside to fling a catfish on the grill for a man whose license plate read Tennessee. Mr. Patrick paid for that, too.

That's when Katie went into the ladies' room around back of the shack to wash her hands.

Soon's I heard her yell, I ran up there and pushed the door hard. Two dark legs poked out from the stall closest to the entrance. Cassie Sharp was bracing herself against its open door with her right arm. The floor was all wet, like maybe a pipe had burst or the toilet overflowed.

Cassie groaned, "Oh Lord, my Lord."

"Cassie!" I gasped.

She looked up at me, then squeezed her eyes shut. She was leanin' against the toilet, her head touchin' the edge of the seat.

"Got to get to Reverend Makepeace..." She grabbed her swollen stomach. "...get to the colored hospital."

"Be right back," I said, and ran out.

I banged into Tad.

"Call Doctor Prout," I said. "Hurry! It's Cassie Sharp."

Tad went for Sam's phone and I went back into the bathroom. Right away, Sam came in, too.

"Jesus," he said.

He ran out. Pretty soon I heard furniture scraping on the concrete.

I wet some paper towels and handed them to Cassie. She wiped her eyes and face. But every time she went to speak, she cringed again.

Then Sam and Tad burst in at once, with Mr. Patrick peering behind them.

"You two squeeze yourselves in there," Sam said to Tad and me. "Grab her on top."

We held our breaths and got either side of the toilet.

Mr. Patrick let his cane fall, took groaning Cassie by one of her legs, grunting himself.

"Don't slip now," Sam told him.

The four of us lifted her, me and Tad her shoulders, Sam and Mr. Patrick her legs. We brought her out to the picnic table Sam must've dragged right up to the bathroom door. His beach blanket with the orange lobster was already spread over it. We set Cassie down.

"Easy," Sam said, "easy."

Cassie moved her head back and forth, squeezed her hands into fists every time a pain came. I stood by her head hopin' the baby wouldn't get born yet.

Tad went back in for Mr. Patrick's cane. He had to wipe it on the grass from the water inside the bathroom.

Mr. Patrick took it from him, then walked away.

"No place for a White man to be," he muttered.

He started for the car.

Doctor Prout squealed into the lot past him in his mamma's white Cadillac she'd used only to go to the The

Links. He leapt out and grabbed his doctor's bag from the back seat. Mamma was with him, too, and Katie ran to her.

"The nigger lady was trying to have her baby in our bathroom!" she said.

Mamma took Katie's face in her hands. "You help me now, Katie, run on over to the rectory and tell Father you need some sheets—towels and sheets."

Sam and Tad moved away from the table to make room for Doctor Prout.

"I'll keep the kids occupied," said Tad, and he waved to some little ones over by the other side of the fish shack. Pretty soon they were singin' "Over There."

I stood over Cassie's head and mopped her face with wet paper towels.

"Mrs. Castleberry's son," she said before she clenched her fists again.

"Yes," Doctor Prout answered. "And you must be Mrs. Sharp. I believe you help Mrs. Haldecott around her place."

He spoke softly to her, looked into her eyes, took her hand and then her other when she squeezed again. I thought of the words he told me his father had said to him. "People have to trust you. You've got to gain their trust." Cassie licked her lips and nodded up at his face. He let her grab his arm and dig her nails in when she squeezed again. Then, without her hardly noticing, he checked her pulse and listened to her heart. His hands moved from one part of her body to another, fast and gentle. He never once lifted them off. Kept talking. Mrs. Sharp, he called her, always Mrs. Sharp.

Mamma went into the kitchen with Sam, then came back with a checkered tablecloth to cover Cassie. Then she got some chair cushions from the inside furniture for pillows. I lifted Cassie's head so Mamma could slip them underneath.

"I was walking to the colored hospital," Cassie panted. "Couldn't make it. Earl... away. Driving."

"Yes, I see he's driving for Mr. Owens."

Cassie grabbed both sides of the picnic table and gasped.

"Fine man, your husband," Doctor Prout continued.

He looked at his watch and counted to himself.

"Yes, sir," she tried to say through gritted teeth.

Doctor Prout had Mamma pour alcohol over his hands. He shook them, then bowed under the red and white tablecloth. Cassie drew up her knees. Mamma stood behind him, holdin' both edges of the cloth like the maid of honor does a wedding train. Cassie groaned and prayed.

Doctor Prout lifted his head back out the tent and whispered something to Mamma. She let the cloth drop and went into the kitchen again.

"You are just about ready to have yourself a baby, Mrs. Sharp," Doctor Prout said. "No need to hurry you anywhere now. This baby wants to be born right here. Appears to be in a hurry. You certainly will have an interesting story to tell this little one and..."

Doctor Prout talked to her like he had nothin' else to do. They could've been rocking on a porch drinking tea. But all the time he was reaching into his bag for instruments and checking to make sure she was alright. My own heart pounded just to watch her flinch. But his voice kept a calm rhythm. A counterpoint, Mrs. Castleberry would have called it, to Cassie's pains.

"Jesus, Lord!" Cassie screamed loud.

I trembled. Father Carriere came running from across the street with Katie. They both held linens in their hands. Sam had them lay the stuff on his counter so they'd be ready for Mamma to take them to Doctor Prout when he told her. Then Father Carriere led Katie back toward the road.

"I'm going to get my mamma," she said, and ran.

Mamma came back with a pan of hot water, a bar of soap, and a clean rag.

"Thank you," Doctor Prout said.

He took the pan, laid it on the ground right under him, soaped the rag, and went under the tablecloth again. Mamma and me looked at one another across the table. Her eyes told me to be strong. Doctor Prout came out, got some orange bottle out the bag and poured whatever it was all over Cassie's stomach and legs. Her body shook and shivered, clenched and unclenched as she panted hard.

"Breathe with Minerva," Doctor Prout said. "In and out, Mrs. Sharp, she'll breathe with you. She knows how to do this."

I stared at Mamma, thinking of her birthing me, how it must have hurt. Wondered if somebody held her hands.

I squeezed my legs together, felt my own privates clench inside. Didn't think I wanted babies if getting them into the world was hard as this.

"Lord have mercy!" Cassie shouted, her head straining back into my hands.

She reached back and grabbed my wrists, clenched them the way Sheriff's metal handcuffs must, but living, hot.

Mamma drew in her own breath, said, "Hold it, Cassie, hold it until you hear ten.

Over and over.

Doctor Prout nodded from below. His voice never wavered.

"Fine, Mrs. Sharp, you are doing just fine. It won't be too long now."

A crowd was gathering—Mrs. Cowles back with Katie, Mrs. Carroll from her store, Father Carriere's housekeeper. Tad had the little kids ringing-around-the-rosie. Siren sounded, loud first, closer and closer, then wound down to a wail as Sheriff Powell stepped out from his car and took the flashing light off the top.

"Nigger's havin' a baby," the man from Tennessee said.

He'd been sitting at the table closest to the road reading a newspaper after he ate, then laid himself on one of the benches to rest "before driving near to Atlanta as I can get today."

Sheriff Powell looked at us, then back at the folks forming a circle just back of the rope near a sign that said, "Line forms here."

"Let's give Doc some privacy," he said.

He spread out his arms and walked toward the group, herding them back toward the road.

"Lord!" Cassie bellowed. "Jesus, have mercy!"

I couldn't feel my wrists, only her grip. Grunting, pushing, squeezing, squealing, an animal caught in a trap, Cassie made her baby come. I heard a slippery burst, smelled hot blood, then squalling, a bleat, and, after a quiet that felt dark as a hole, a steady new cry.

Tears sprung out my eyes. Cassie let go my wrists. There was blood where her nails had dug in.

"Thank you," she said. "Thank you, Lord."

Her voice was dripping wet, a heavy load of joy.

Doctor Prout stood up under the tablecloth, arms full. Mamma lifted the edges and flung them off his head. He held a baby covered all over in something soft and crumbly white that Mamma wiped away with a lobster bib.

Then she got a folded sheet from the counter and held it out so Doctor Prout could lay the baby in her arms. He hovered over her, examining the squalling child, head and ears first, then the mouth, clearing it with his finger. He touched hands and toes, then, satisfied, nodded to Mamma, who wrapped and wrapped the sheet around the infant and walked to the side of the table to hand the bundle at last to Cassie's open arms.

"A girl," Doctor Prout said.

Sounded like Amen.

He came around to me and stroked Cassie's forehead.

"You have birthed a beautiful baby girl, Mrs. Sharp."

She grabbed his hands over the bundle.

"Thank you," she said. "Your mamma raised you good."

Doctor Prout stood all the way up. He was drenched in sweat and smiling down at her.

"I'll just finish up now while you enjoy your baby," he said, and ducked under the tablecloth again.

I watched Mamma watching him. Her eyes bore through the cloth as he pressed and pushed on Cassie's stomach. I came around the table, stood by Mamma, when something else dripping slipped out of Cassie, and Doctor Prout caught it and examined it in his hands. After a while he dropped it, dark and hot and red into the soapy pan.

"Looks whole," he said to himself.

I had no idea what it was.

His arms and hands and shirt were dripping blood when he faced us. Mamma held out a towel. He took it, wiped his hands, and brought it to his face. When he let it fall, he looked again.

He was wet and glowing, like he had come to life.

Cassie crooned behind us.

"Baby," she said, "my own sweet girl."

We all turned and watched. The little girl's mouth moved, already looking for milk.

"You did a good job," Mamma said.

She put her hand on Doctor Prout's red arm.

I closed my eyes, remembered the warmth of his hand on my shoulder. How I had to wait until I was nearly eleven-and-a-half before I felt it. How I wanted to feel it now.

I opened my eyes, looked over to Mamma, then at him again.

"Fa-ther?" I said, testing the word, feeling my tongue touch my teeth, learning to speak all over again.

Mamma bit her lip to bleeding and watched my face.

"Yes," he answered, his eyes tearing. "A very bad one."

I looked at the face, a mirror of my own. Our mouths tried to still themselves. Something bigger than opera or Christmas grew inside my chest. Something even my brush would find hard to describe. I was Easter and fireworks, last day of school. Crying out loud and winning the race. Promise and dread. Waiting, forgotten. Now and good-bye.

A sigh came up from my middle, rose to throat. Then out of my mouth it unfurled, mixed with the air grown thick in the heat.

By themselves, without my knowing, my hands reached to his. Then, like he'd been waiting, he stood up full and gathered us both in his arms, Mamma one side, me the other, smearing us red with the mess of new life.

She let him, meeting my eyes across his bloody shirt. Her desperate look searched my face.

I looked back, held her in my gaze, told her with my eyes that I was Orla Gwen, her daughter who somehow would try to forgive her for what she had done.

"The father's away at Pontchartrain," Sheriff Powell interrupted. "Had two bankers to drive around for Owens. Due back tomorrow."

"Hear that, Cassie?" Mamma said, tryin' to find her regular tone. "Your Earl's going to get a nice surprise."

But Cassie didn't answer. I turned my head and saw her and her baby just about asleep.

Doctor Prout still held on. The three of us stood together for the first time, the secret we carried acknowledged at last.

Tad and the little kids yelled, "And we all fall down!" I curled around, pushing Doctor Prout out of the middle and putting myself between Mamma and him. They clasped each other's arms over me, making a cocoon of comfort and shade. I breathed in their sweat. Rubbed my face against their chests. Listened to their hearts. Doctor Prout's chin nuzzled my hair and Mamma stood on tiptoe to kiss his forehead.

"You look like hell," Sam said, surprising us. Then, "Sorry, Minerva, I shouldn't have..."

But Mamma only laughed. The cocoon broke open.

"I guess we could all do with a shower."

Most the folks had gone their own ways, and Sheriff Powell said, "You want me to drive her back to The Hollow?"

"No need now, I guess," said Doctor Prout, pointing.

Reverend and Mrs. Makepeace drove into the lot. Tad ran over to their car. The little kids followed.

Doctor Prout went over and leaned down by Cassie's ear, "I'll be by to see you this evening," he told her.

Mrs. Makepeace leaned over Cassie, too.

"Congratulations, Cassie, I'm sorry we didn't find you in time."

Cassie stirred.

"No matter, Mrs. Makepeace. Mrs. Castleberry's boy did good as his mamma could want. Goin' to call my baby Belle after her. My baby's name is Belle Sharp."

Doctor Prout bowed his head.

"I am most honored," he said.

Then Mrs. Makepeace took the baby and helped Cassie sit up so Reverend Makepeace and Doctor Prout could lift her up and carry her to the reverend's car. Tad saw and came running to help, while the little kids stared after him. Mamma gathered up all the bloody towels and sheets and carried them to the big washing machine back of Sam's kitchen.

"We best burn them, I think," Sam said.

"I guess," Mamma answered.

Then she washed her hands in bleach same as we used at Mrs. Castleberry's to get clothes white.

Doctor Prout came back as the Makepeace's drove away.

Tad hollered over to him, "My dad's expecting me over at the office. He thinks I've been up at your place."

Doctor Prout mopped his head with one of the lobster bibs. "Thank you, Tad," he said, "you were a great help."

Tad turned as he started to sprint. "All in a day's work in St. Suplice," he laughed.

Sam put his hands on his hips and surveyed his picnic patio. "Beer?" he asked.

Doctor Prout sat on the picnic bench and leaned back onto the table that was itself again. He stuck his legs out and looked at the sky. Long, he was, my father was long.

"A six-pack will do," he said.

Mamma smiled.

"We've been needin' a doctor for a long time," Sam said.

He snapped open a beer can and handed it to Doctor Prout.

"You gonna stay?"

Mamma looked at Doctor Prout, who stared at me.

Sam opened two more beers, one for Mamma, the other for himself. Gave me a cream soda.

"We'll see, Sam," he said, and took a gulp.

My heart somersaulted. Mamma looked at the ground. Then a *Times Picayune* truck pulled into the lot and Mr. Cowles got out.

"Heads up," Sam said, and we drank. He downed his beer real quick, while Mr. Cowles was still adjusting his pants, and Doctor Prout disappeared around back.

Mr. Cowles walked up to the counter.

"What'll it be, my man?" asked Sam, walking toward him.

Mr. Cowles adjusted his belt.

"Depends."

He looked over at Doctor Prout's bag still on the ground. Picked at his teeth with a toothpick.

"True my Katie found a nigger woman in the bathroom? True Castleberry delivered a nigger baby in broad daylight so my little girl saw?" Mr. Cowles asked what he already knew. Moved his head like the lion came on the screen before the movie.

Sam handed him a beer.

"On the house," he said.

Sam turned his baseball cap around backwards. Mr. Cowles downed the beer in a series of gulps. Then he wiped his mouth with the back of his hand.

"Well?" he said. He scratched his face that needed a shave.

Sam looked at him and said, "Never had no need to lock them doors all these years, Mr. Cowles. I wonder when she skulked in. Must've been before I arrived this morning."

He spoke in a tired voice that knew it didn't matter what he said.

Mr. Cowles scratched his head. Put the toothpick into his breast pocket.

"Point is," he said, slow and drawn out, "I don't want my Katie seeing some sorry nigger's filthy privates."

Sam put his hands on the counter and leaned over it, closer to Mr. Cowles.

"And I don't want you talking like that in front of this girl, neither," he said.

Mr. Cowles looked over at Mamma and me and gave a snort.

"Them are nigger lovers," he said.

Mamma's face tightened and she stood up.

"Don't you dare," she said.

I knew she'd let him bloody her nose and still fight back.

I stood up, too.

"Shut up," I said, just over a whisper. "Just shut up."

Mamma didn't correct me.

Mr. Cowles spit the ground near Mamma, punched the beer can with a fist, and sent it flyin' right at Sam's face.

"Get outta here," Sam told him, not even botherin' to yell.

"You'll regret this," Mr. Cowles said.

Sam came around the front of the counter. He was short, but thick. A vein bulged out the side of his neck as he pointed his nose under Mr. Cowles' chin.

"You threatening me, Cowles?" he asked.

Mr. Cowles stared down at Sam.

"No, promising," he said, and spit again.

A bubble of phlegm glittered on Sam's shoe, but Sam never flinched. Then Mr. Cowles walked back to the truck, every inch of it exceptin' the driver's seat piled high with copies of the evening edition. He turned on the engine and squealed out the lot fast enough to make little dust tornadoes twirl above the ground.

Sam went back around the counter and picked up the can. He tossed it into the trash.

"Good riddance to the son of a— sorry, he's got me talking like that myself. How a guy like that got Bridget to marry him I'll never know."

He fixed his cap right again, looked around, said, "Hey, where's Prou—" then, running for the kitchen, shouted, "Look out!"

But it was too late. Doctor Prout came around the side of the shack with the hose in his hand. He aimed it right at Mamma and me. The water was a welcome slap that tickled and cooled. We screamed, surprised.

"Get him!" Mamma said.

She grabbed my hand and we ran at him together.

"Hope you're ready," she threatened.

She kicked Doctor Prout right in the shins so he yelped in pain and dropped the wiggling green snake.

"Hold him," she told me, and I did, pulling hard on his slippery arms so he couldn't get loose.

Mamma chased the hose while it jumped and turned, then managed to grab it tight to hand to me.

She stood behind Doctor Prout, holding his arms to her chest.

"Get him," she shouted, so I aimed at his shirt, laughing until he cried, "Uncle! Uncle!"and the concrete ran red.

Not one of us cared who saw.

"You done now?" Sam asked, peering out from the kitchen.

He came out from around the counter, said, "What a day, and it ain't two yet. I'm gonna close early."

Mamma went around the side of the shack and turned off the hose. Sam stared at the bathroom door, then higher. Looked like he saw something wrong with the roof.

"Aw, what the hell," he said to himself, then to Doctor Prout, "Help me, will ya?"

He lugged a ladder out from the kitchen, then made Doctor Prout hold it while he climbed high enough to reach the Whites Only sign.

"Hand me my hammer, Minerva, will you'?" he said. "It's in the drawer under the cash register."

"I'll get it," I said.

I ran into the shack and over to the counter. The hammer lay under a pile of coupons and had rubber bands red and taffy-colored wrapped up and down the handle. Letter opener, too, and a page from a magazine with an advertisement said, "Hair Growth Guaranteed" next to a picture of a lady kissing the top of a man's curly head.

"Be careful," Mamma was sayin' outside.

I ran back and handed the hammer up to Sam. He banged loose the pegs that held the sign in place, let them fall to the ground, then lowered the sign down to Mamma so she could hold it. It had splattered bug parts all over it and some rust, too.

"Don't make no sense now," he said.

Doctor Prout walked back to the picnic table and drank another beer. He lay down on the table, his feet hangin' over the side.

"I would say not," he said.

Simple as that.

"That will cost you some, don't you think, Sam?" Mamma said.

She looked serious.

Sam looked up at the space empty now, then over at the sign, then at Mamma's eyes.

"See any other food stands in town?" He laughed.

He went for the trash with the sign.

"Wait," I said. "Tad will want it, for sure."

Sam handed it to me and I put it next to Doctor Prout's bag.

"Maybe when Cowles gets through with me, my insurance will let me retire, anyway," he said.

Mamma squeezed water out of her hair, then said, "What will the rest of us do? I would sorely miss your fried shrimp."

She said it like she was talking about something solemn.

"Big ones, I got big ones today," Sam said.

They went into the kitchen. Doctor Prout lay across the picnic table and closed his eyes.

I was alone again, but not really. Grammie's crucifix on my throat was all crooked from the spray, so I fixed it and felt it rest against my neck again like always. But Grammie wasn't my grandmother anymore.

I felt shaky. The air waved in front of my eyes. My brain felt too big for my head.

I couldn't tell her. That would be worse than sayin' good-bye at the pier had been—her cryin' and me and Mamma waving We love you, good-bye, until we couldn't see the ship at all. What was the point of the truth, anyway, if it wrecked a body's life?

I walked over to the horse chestnut with the tire swing. Mamma and Sam were singin' "That's my baby now." The road was empty in the mid-day heat. Doctor Prout snored.

An idea was forming in my mind that maybe false and true are too small for anything but history tests. Maybe sometimes it's alright to lie. Maybe sometimes a body even should. But when? I fingered the cross in my hands.

Dear Grammie, I'd write, *Today a Negro lady had a baby right on a picnic table at Sam's. I helped.*

And she'd be happy. She'd put my letter back into its envelope said Air Mail and kiss the return address like she used to with the cards from her brothers. Then after tea before she went to bed, she'd sit down in her rocker, take my letter out, and read it again.

Plus, I couldn't stop thinking of her as my grandmother anyway. Wouldn't want to. Wasn't for her, Mamma wouldn't have been able to earn any money after my Daddy died. Practically every song I knew I learned from her. That and sewing hems, too.

I brought her cross to my lips and kissed it. Thought of the lies Mamma had told me, the ones I knew of, anyway. Necessary lies they must have been. A body didn't tell a lie for nothing.

I grabbed the sides of the tire and pulled myself up into its center. I let my sandals drop and pumped my legs hard till I was flying eye to eye with birds. I felt the sun dryin' me off, smelled the shrimp crackling in the grease made them tasty, heard Sam and Mamma talkin' like it was an ordinary day. Pretty soon, Doctor Prout's arms dropped over the sides of the picnic table.

Happily ever after is how I wanted to feel. A girl swinging in a tree. Her parents nearby. A bathroom for anyone needed it now. A hose for fun, besides.

But I knew that was just a fairy tale. I couldn't escape the truth about Grammie and my Daddy who really wasn't.

A bird most hit my face. Came so close I tasted feathers on my lips. The tire spun while I shook them off. Sheriff Powell's car sped by, the light on its roof flashing and spinning. I started pumping again.

Doctor Prout will likely go back to Boston and I'll be so angry I'll want to kill him when what I really want is for him to stay. Mamma will hate him even though she loves him, too. I'll be without my second daddy, this time knowin' my name is wrong besides. I'll live in a beautiful house surrounded by things that remind me of who I should have been, but nobody'll be there to be related to and Mamma will do the laundry the same as before. Mr. Cowles will wreck Sam's place, for sure. Spit at little Belle Sharp just for bein' born a color folks decided is wrong.

"Ready," Mamma announced, and carried a tray outside.

Doctor Prout sat up slowly, rubbed his eyes, eased himself down onto the picnic bench, and breathed in the shrimp. Mamma tied a clean lobster bib around his neck.

"Want any, Orla?" Sam yelled, as I pumped and pumped.

"No, thanks," I answered.

It was enough to watch, to pretend it was really mine, to breathe it all in, and save the scene for my canvas. Full is how I felt, anyway, full of something I might be close to having, even though I knew I was taking a big chance. But hope was what I felt now and feeling it was good. So I took a deep breath, threw back my head, stretched out my legs as far as they could reach, and pumped harder and harder long as I could stand to.

Chapter Thirty-Two

We stopped at our place and packed some clothes and paints, took Mrs. Castleberry's record player, too, and got back to the big house to hear Miss Yvette talkin' to the Italians on the telephone.

"I'm going to learn to drive," Mamma said, as Doctor Prout started the car.

He looked sideways at her.

"Why?" he asked. "Planning on going somewhere?"

Mamma looked back at him like a waterfall was spouting out his head.

"To pick up the lace, of course, to take Orla to school with the Ursulines, to drive the women from The Hollow to the house for lessons."

She straightened her blouse.

"To get my hair cut, maybe, too."

Doctor Prout stared at her hair around her shoulders.

"Yvette and I decided your father's old medical office will make a good workshop."

Doctor Prout didn't respond, just stared straight ahead.

"And if you like, Orla," Mamma continued, "we'll call the place Easels and Lace. We'll show your work. Yvette thinks it can be a real gallery."

I leaned forward and rested my chin on Mamma's seat from the back.

"To sell it, you mean? People payin' for my paintings?"

Mamma turned to me and smiled.

"Why not?" she said. "Why ever not?"

Doctor Prout waved to Father Carriere, who was pacing back and forth in front of the rectory.

"But what if I decide to leave Boston, open a practice here?" he said.

He smiled, but he didn't seem happy.

My heart fluttered. I looked from him to Mamma and back again.

Mamma cleared her throat and spoke like Miss Foster did before a test.

"The two of us can't wait for you to decide what you're doing before we plan the rest of our lives."

Doctor Prout stepped on the brake and we jolted, Mamma 'bout hitting her head on the dashboard. I grabbed her back by the shoulders.

"Mr. Patrick's going to teach me. We'll use the station wagon."

Doctor Prout turned on the radio. Couldn't hear anything but static.

"Bad reception," he said, like he was telling us something we didn't know.

Mamma turned back to me.

"What do you think?" she said.

I imagined the waiting room and the old office painted lavender and sage green. My paintings on wooden easels between hangers of lace blouses, a wedding dress, some detachable cuffs and collars, and a baptismal gown or two. We'd set a table for tea, with Mrs. Castleberry's prettiest china, and there'd always be flowers just cut from the garden.

"Yes," I said.

Mamma turned off the radio. Doctor Prout looked at her sideways again, then drove faster.

"Good," Mamma said.

I sat back in my seat.

"We'll talk to Yvette about it tonight."

When we pulled into the drive, Doctor Prout got right out of the car, went inside without waiting, and closed the door behind him in his daddy's study.

The phone rang. Miss Yvette picked up and, all of a sudden, she was speaking another language.

"*Si, si,*" she said.

She covered the receiver and whispered to Mamma, "They received the telegram early this morning."

She turned away again.

"*È vero.*"

She wrote fast in pencil on the notepad.

"*Alora, il ventisei luglio. Va bene.*"

She looked back at us and waved her hand up and down, made a question mark with her hand.

"*Anche noi.*"

Mamma and me looked at her notes.

"They're arriving July 26," she whispered.

I looked at Mamma.

"But that's when I go to New York," I said.

She nodded.

"No," I turned to the veranda and kicked at the air.

"Come on," Mamma motioned, and went outside.

I folded my hands across my chest.

"But I won't see them," I said.

Mamma sat down on the steps and patted the top one for me to do the same.

"You will, silly," she said. "You'll only be gone for two days. Then you can come back with Miss Yvette. They'll stay until Gabriella leaves for The Julliard, anyway."

I wanted to meet them at the pier, to see if Doctor Prout and his sister looked alike. My father. My aunt. The three of us together.

"Promise you won't do anything fun," I looked at Mamma. "Swear."

She laughed. "Scout's honor." She raised her right hand.

"*Ci vediamo*," Miss Yvette said. "*Buon viaggio!*"

Miss Yvette hung up and turned to come outside. She opened her mouth to speak, then looked at Mamma and me from head to toe.

"What on earth happened?" she said.

Chapter Thirty-Three

Mamma and Miss Yvette went into the kitchen. I knew they'd make cocktails and eventually we'd have supper. Right now I just wanted to be alone.

I went upstairs to Mrs. Castleberry's room to shower. I guess I wasn't sneaking since she'd willed us to live here. I picked up a picture of her in a gold frame with a metal bow that looked just-tied on top of it. She was in her school uniform in France. I held it next to my face and studied us side by side in her bureau mirror. Our noses pretty much matched.

Then I sat down in the seat she called her slipper chair, arranged my legs the way she did hers. But mine just looked like sticks.

I heard Mamma and Miss Yvette go out onto the veranda and clink their glasses.

I walked over to Mrs. Castleberry's bed bigger than my whole room at our old house and lay down. It felt the way I imagined a cloud would, the kind Miss Foster called cumulus. Had two pillows each one long as a laundry sack.

They cradled my head so it nestled in cotton. I closed my eyes. Disappeared into white. Empty. Peaceful. Gone.

When my eyes opened to Mamma's voice, my tongue felt thick with sleep.

"Here you are," she said.

She smelled of liquor. Sat down beside me. The white cloud rolled.

"So now you know," she said.

Her voice was kind and a little bit sad.

I didn't say anything.

"More than you think," I said.

She stared out the window for a while, then looked back down at me.

"I had to give us a name, you see, to make us respectable."

She said it calm, matter of fact.

But then she shook her head, got bitter as vinegar.

"There is nothing more important in St. Suplice than respectability."

She sounded snotty now. Mrs. Allaire, only younger.

I turned on my side and looked out the window. Imagined my Daddy holding me, believing I was his. Building my crib, carving my initials *OGG* into wood he had cut himself.

"Can you imagine how we would have been treated?"

I sucked my hand. Trollop was what Mrs. Haldecott called Billy Carroll's cousin Meg had no ring on her finger and brought her baby boy to visit. Mamma told me what it meant. What folks would've called Fern Mae if she hadn't been slow.

"Did he know?"

Mamma leaned on the bed with one elbow.

"I don't know," she said, then, "You mean Sean?"

I looked back inside, up at her face.

"Both of them."

Mamma sat straight up again.

"I never told Prout. I couldn't once I was married."

I turned on my other side and the cloud gave way.

"So you lied to him, too."

"Yes, I lied."

I sat up. I was furious. I smacked the pillow.

"You would have just kept lying."

Smacked the pillow again.

"Why?" I yelled, "How could you lie to me?"

I hit her arm so hard my own hand stung.

Mamma's face went tight. She grabbed my hand and squeezed it hard.

"So no one," her voice turned wet and heavy, "so *no one* would call you a bastard child."

She let go, then put her head in her hands and sobbed.

I watched, glad to see her suffer.

The study door opened and closed downstairs. The grandfather clock chimed five. A motorcycle roared out on the road.

Mamma lifted her head, wiped her eyes and spoke again.

"So she would have to see you every day, learn how wonderful you are," she almost smiled. Then she whispered, like she was sayin' something holy, "So she would want you for her own."

Mamma started crying again. I watched her get up and pull a tissue from the silver box on the nightstand. She wiped her eyes and blew her nose.

Then, all of a sudden, she got strong. She clenched her right fist and punched the air.

"And it worked," she said. "By God, Orla, I succeeded. She came to love you, loved you more than anyone else."

Mamma smiled a big smile, then brought down her fist, opened her hand, and put it to her throat, lifting her chin like she was trying to keep her head from falling off.

Her smile disappeared.

"She took him away from me first."

Mamma's eyelids fluttered up and down and her voice sounded wavy.

"Now," then Mamma dropped onto the bed beside me, "now she's taken you, too."

She put her hand to her mouth to keep the scream in.

I gasped.

"Mamma," I cried, "Mamma."

I took her arms and made her look at me. She looked sadder than I'd ever seen. Her face was almost as white as the coverlet. Tears ran out her eyes and onto the bed and she lay all tired out, limp and worn. I stroked her arm, her hair. Got another tissue, blotted her cheeks.

Finally she spoke again.

First she whispered, "But you'll never have to worry."

Then she raised herself up. She arched her back, thrust out her chin.

Like she was telling the world, she announced, "You'll be free. You're free, Orla, don't you see?"

Her eyes glistened. Her hands parted the air. She became beautiful and wild. And I knew she'd done it for me.

The ceiling fan whirred and stirred the fragrant roses by the bed. Mamma kissed and kissed my cheeks. Her fingers caressed my neck. Then, suddenly, she let go, fell down again on the bed, turned on her side, and drew her knees to her chest. We snuggled against each other close, rocking on Mrs. Castleberry's bed. The two of us again, but different than before.

Chapter Thirty-Four

After I showered, I got my paints out from where our workshop would be, Dr. Castleberry's old office just behind the kitchen and other side of the mud room. I set my easel away from the house looking toward the road. So many pictures I needed to paint, but the one that came to my brush first was a butterfly spreading her wings out from a cocoon dropping.

I painted her big, not the butterfly against a background, but the background barely behind the butterfly. Her edges ran off the canvas so drops of paint fell on the grass. I couldn't contain her. Mostly her wings were loud, lemon-rind yellow, with bits of black and tiny lines of red, like veins of leaves. To make her move, I brushed in dandelion puffs falling and a wisp of grey-white bird feathers. Later her body would look black from far away, but close up, I folded in deepest brown and crimson made me think of loam and soil wet enough to nurture seeds without a rain.

I rubbed my fingers in the paint. I smudged on purpose here and there, dirtying her wings with bits of brown and orange, yellowing her center near the tip, narrowing her pointy bottom with black, black.

Everything was running into everything else, extending the edges, making one color blend with another.

Same was happening to me. All summer long I'd been tryin' to figure out this or that, either and or. But it didn't work. At least not for me. Or Mamma, either, or Mrs. Castleberry, or even Doctor Prout. He no more knew he had a sister named after an angel than I had been able to figure out why Mamma had married a man she didn't love. Everything was a puzzle with pieces fitting a little at a time, and some of them missing, maybe forever.

I flicked my fingernails at the wings' edges, leaving thin-flecked lines of space where outline used to be. Unfinished.

That's how a body's life must be. All the time waiting, knowing and not knowing, understanding and trying to figure things out. Wanting. Having sometimes, but knowing without, expecting without again.

I sat back and looked at the butterfly. It is a fact, like rain is wet or two plus two equals four. I made it myself. It stares back at me. Yes, Orla, this is the way the world looks. I feel sure. Powerful and sure.

"Orla," I hear his voice reaching, "I'm grilling some steak."

He doesn't sound angry, but how can a body tell?

I look away from the painting and towards the porch. I want to answer, say *Father*. But I don't.

"Coming," I say.

I gather my paints, lift the easel, carry it all into the used-to-be medical office, and come back outside.

Miss Yvette stands up first. She clicks down the steps to meet me.

"You've had quite a day, I hear," she says.

I face her, waiting for which parts she means.

She leans close to my hair and with her bangled hand moves it gently away from my ear.

"Tante. You may call me Tante Yvette."

Then she kisses me on both cheeks like Mrs. Castleberry told me, "the way the French do, my dear."

Chapter Thirty-Five

"I'll go with you," I said to Doctor Prout.

It was past eight. We all felt ourselves again. Mamma was ready to work with Miss Yvette and me on the lace catalog, but she nodded alright to Doctor Prout as he got his bag ready and took the keys off the foyer table.

They'd hardly talked at supper.

"Have you ever been to The Hollow? he asked.

We got into the station wagon.

"No," I said. I felt my heart fluttering. "Is this like rounds?"

He started the car.

"Exactly."

Night was coming on. He drove slowly now, and I could watch the orange-pink sky slip into lilac and then to grey. We passed our little house all closed up and waved to Lizzy and Mrs. Crowther playin' cards on the porch. The Carroll boys moved out of the way, their baseball rolling slowly in the road till we passed. Mr. and Mrs. Cowles were sitting on their front stoop. He smoked a cigar and she knitted. When she waved, he pulled at her arm. Katie was playin' hopscotch with one of the Ferrier girls. No sign of Denny.

A light shone out of Father Carriere's study and I saw his shadow reading. Tad's grandpa and his friends were playin' cards outside Crossroads Cinema, where the marquee said, Closed for Repairs until Further Notice. Some mangy dog I didn't recognize sniffed into the grass by Carroll's Sundries, and Mrs. Allaire rocked on her porch, her chin on her chest, unaware we were driving by.

Had to go all the way through town and then out from it till the road turned from cement to gravel, and finally became a path mostly walked on into The Hollow.

"No place for White people," Mr. Patrick always said, whenever Father Carriere went there with Reverend Makepeace. "Don't know why Old Doc Castleberry bothered. The niggers never paid him cash."

I thought how Doctor Prout called Cassie "Mrs. Sharp." Didn't hear him ask her for money.

He shifted down into second gear. Took care to go slow. Watched that no one was walking in front of us. The path was rutted, and ferns and weeds grew tall each side of it. Trees and bushes never been trimmed or cut down made night earlier than back in town. Insects and birds sawed and screeched. Something black flew over the hood of the car. Eyes not human stared from the thick.

"Did you come here with your daddy?" I tried to sound unafraid.

Doctor Prout looked over at me.

"You alright?" he asked.

I hadn't noticed both my hands gripping the seat, how I sat forward, peering hard into the windshield.

"Billy Carroll said no White girl ever came in here got out alive."

Doctor Prout nodded.

"Next time you see him, you tell Billy what you saw. I'll confirm whatever you say."

His voice made me feel better, but my hands still held onto the seat.

We came out from the long path was really a tunnel into a clearing. A circle of houses looked more like cabins were grouped together, each one a little different from the next. One had a bench out front filled with flower pots and an old lady in a long skirt watering. It was the same one who had been on the altar, the one who knew magic. An old man might've been her husband sat on the step by her. He tipped his straw hat as Doctor Prout slowed and waved.

"Thought I'd see how Mrs. Sharp is doing," Doctor Prout said so anyone could hear.

He pulled up to the third cabin and turned off the engine.

"Coming?" he asked.

I nodded, and Doctor Prout got his bag, came around the car, opened the door, and helped me out. I saw candles flickering in one of the windows, and heard a little voice complaining, "I don't want to go to sleep." Someone laughed in the woods, and water splashed from a bucket somewhere I couldn't see.

"Orla and I have come to visit," Doctor Prout said very loudly, as he walked up the steps.

Then he knocked.

"It's open," I heard Cassie's voice.

He let me in first and I had to blink. There was only one light, over the old-fashioned stove, icebox, and sink. The whole cabin was just one room. Cassie was lyin' in a bed, but crosswise, so she could lean against the wall. She had a turban on her head now, and little Belle was swaddled in white cotton. There was a cup of water on a little table had

233

been pushed close to the bed, and a dish used to have food that had been eaten already. A crumbled napkin held the fork and knife. The room smelled like chopped wood and orange peels. A man's clothes were hung neatly from pegs on the wall, and a cradle waited for Belle next to the big bed.

"How are you doing, Mrs. Sharp?" Doctor Prout asked.

Already he had put down his bag, opened it, spread out a clean towel, and put some instruments on it. He looked around the room, studying it, like he'd have a test on it later.

"Fine, fine," Cassie said. "Mrs. Makepeace came by earlier, and the other ladies keep dropping by to make sure we're well."

Doctor Prout looked into her eyes with a flashlight, listened to her chest, then helped her set Belle down on the bed.

I stood back, thinking how our little house was a palace compared to this, wondering where a body could get comfortable here. Two wooden chairs, a wooden table in the kitchen, and the bed were the only places a body could sit or rest. I couldn't see a radio or a phone. Saw a few books on one of the windowsills. *The Holy Bible*, a State of Louisiana Driver's Manual, and *Ways to Improve Your Earning Power*.

Belle squirmed on the bed while Doctor Prout checked her.

"Keep the cord very clean," he said. "It'll fall off by itself."

Cassie nodded and smiled. "I been taking care of babies for a long time, Doctor," she said. "This time it's finally one of my own."

Doctor Prout wrapped Belle up again and handed her to her mamma. Soon as Cassie turned to adjust her pillow against the wall, he reached into his bag, took out an envelope said *Congratulations* in his handwriting on the front and slipped it under the dish on the table.

"When do you expect Earl?" he asked.

Cassie turned back to him.

"Tomorrow evening," she said.

Doctor Prout began to pack his things.

"Well, you be sure to have him come and get me if you have any concerns."

Cassie nodded, stretched out her legs, and opened her robe to nurse Belle.

I heard steps outside. The cabin door opened and the magic lady came in with a pot she put on the stove. It smelled sweet and tangy at the same time.

"Good evening," Doctor Prout said.

The old woman turned and paused.

"I knew your mother," she said.

"Yes," Doctor Prout answered.

"I am sorry that she passed," she said. "She meant well."

Doctor Prout tried to keep composed.

"Thank you, Ma'am," he said.

"And who is this?" she pointed to me. Her hands were gnarled and her voice raspy.

I felt naked, displayed.

Doctor Prout put his arm around my shoulders. I held my breath, breathed in the just-black night, heard Belle suck and Cassie croon.

"This is her grandchild, Ma'am. This is Orla, my daughter."

The woman came close to my face.

"Yes," she said. "I see."

My eyes glistened, then filled. I felt as deep as the river. Moving, the current inside me taking me places I'd never been. The woman patted my hand. Her touch felt like a spell.

"Why, I didn't know—" Cassie began, then stopped.

Doctor Prout turned back toward her. She lowered her eyes and held Belle tighter.

"You enjoy your little girl, now, Mrs. Sharp," he said, "while I get mine back home before her mother tells me I've kept her out too late."

I grabbed his hand and we walked into the night. Most every porch was lit by candles. Doctor Prout helped me into the car, then went around to his side, got in, and started the engine. He backed the car into the open space, then turned it around to face away from the cabins.

"Good night," he called out.

"Yessir," a man's voice answered.

And we made our way out the dark tunnel.

I turned in my seat and looked back. My skin felt new. The candles on the porches glowed behind, their light dimming little by little, then disappearing completely as we headed back to town. Seemed like a curtain closed, like The Hollow had never really existed.

"What would you like to call me, anyway?" Doctor Prout asked, as the tires met gravel again.

I tried to speak, but my voice caught. The road was uneven, so I held on to the armrest to keep from sliding.

He kept driving. The tires moved from gravel to cement. Time we passed St. Marguerite's, he had picked up speed.

St. Suplice looked the way it did most every night—small, still, its ugly parts hidden by the dark. But everything felt different. I had gone into The Hollow half an orphan and come back out with my father alive. I rubbed my hand where the old lady had touched it.

We passed Sam's, the park, then came to the bend that led to the Castleberry place.

"Well?" he asked. "What will you call me?"

I didn't know what to say, so I pretended I was holding my paintbrush.

"Doctor Prout," I said.

The car slowed. He looked across the seat at me.

"That's what you call me now," he said.

The wheels rolled over something soft, squishy, maybe still alive.

"I know," I said.

I tried to keep my voice even.

His voice got softer. Smooth.

"But things are different now, aren't they, now that you know who I really am?"

I felt queasy and had to swallow more than once.

"Not really," I said.

He pulled to the side of the road, turned off the ignition, draped his arm over his seat.

My heart pounded.

Doctor Prout rubbed his chin with his hand. Traced the steering wheel with his fingers.

"Why not?" he asked.

My brush could have told him a million reasons. How he'd never asked Mamma if I was his. That he'd never come to see me or sent a card. When, even at his daddy's funeral, he wasn't curious enough to find me, to see if I looked like him. I would have painted an empty house with window sills that frowned, a man escaping out the back door, running sideways against the wind.

"Because," I began.

Then tears ran quickly down my face.

"Here," he said, like he was giving me a present, and took a handkerchief from his pocket.

"Because," I started again, and I thought of who my grandmother was.

I sat up straight in my seat, held my legs together like she did, put my hands in my lap.

"Because," I said, "a person doesn't leave blood. No matter what. And you did."

He switched on the overhead light. He didn't look angry or sad or anything at all.

"You're right," he said, "I did."

I took a deep breath and made sure not to move.

He rolled down his window and looked away from me into the night. Something I couldn't see screeched deep in the brush.

Turning back, he said, "I don't think Mother could share me. I stayed away so she couldn't lock me in."

I kept still, felt how heavy night was. Heard my own breaths come, one after the other. Nothing more to say.

"And so, very selfishly, I abandoned you, your mother and you."

I looked at the windshield. Insects crawled across it and something grunting scurried across the road.

"I wish I could buy back time, make it up to you both."

I didn't look at him.

"But you can't," I said.

He took a deep breath.

"What would you have me do, then?"

It was my only chance.

I dug my nails into the upholstery, tried to figure out how I could hate and tell him at the same time, stared straight ahead, and said, "Stay. I want you to stay."

Hot needles pricked me from inside my chest. My eyes turned kaleidoscopes, and I breathed fast, afraid the air would run out.

My father reached over his hand and held it top of my head. Kept me from falling in a heap. Rubbed my curls.

238

Chapter Thirty-Six

Mr. Patrick took Mamma over to the church parking lot for her first driving lesson the day Tante Yvette flew back to New York, a week before Doctor Prout was leaving, too.

"I'll meet you at the airport on the twenty-sixth," she told me, while Earl Sharp put her suitcase into the back. "I'll have some new things for you to try on, too."

Three days before she left we had spent most of the time deciding which of my paintings to ship to the show. We decided on a Freedom Rider bus blowin' up, my butterfly, the scene of Doctor Prout and me on the dock, and Mamma slapping Mrs. Castleberry's rug out her bedroom window.

Every day Mamma got excited about learning some new thing—backing into parking spaces, parallel parking outside Mr. Carroll's store, passing on the left when the painted white lines separated.

"I certainly will not marry him," she told me at breakfast right after her first day on the real road, "at least not until he behaves like a father for one whole year."

I had been eating cereal in the kitchen. Doctor Prout was playing golf at The Links with Tad and his daddy.

"But you already act like he's your husband," I said.

Mamma stopped scooping the seeds out of a cantaloupe and looked at me.

I took another bite of cereal, then licked the spoon and tapped it on the side of the bowl.

"I saw," I said. "Twice."

Mamma stooped and got a roll of tin foil out of the wrap drawer. She stood up, turned the cantaloupe upside down, and dumped the seeds onto the foil, pushing them along with the spoon. She pushed the wrapper drawer in with her knee, then washed her hands at the sink, and turned to look at me.

"What we do by ourselves is none of your business, young lady," she said. "You have no business snooping."

I stirred the cereal, smashing the square-shaped pieces.

Mamma looked angry.

I stared at my feet.

"What if you have a baby?"

Mamma poured a cup of coffee, then came and sat by me.

"So that's what you're worried about, then," she said. She leaned over and kissed me on my head. I pulled away.

She took a long sip of coffee, "There won't be any babies anytime soon, that's for sure. You just stick to your painting and your studies. Your father and I will take care of the rest."

I wanted to say more, to tell her how scared I had been to see them, how it looked like he was killing her, that they'd want a new baby more than me.

"Alright?" Mamma asked.

I nodded, but barely.

"I'm going upstairs to iron the guest room curtains."

I went outside and set up my easel. Brushed stroke after stroke of color for a long time. Gashes of crimson. Drizzling yellow. Splatters of blue I dotted with black. No images, only the way I felt inside, glorious to glum in a minute's time.

240

Whole morning passed and I hardly noticed.

Doctor Prout would be coming back here July twenty-fifth so he could meet his sister at the pier on the twenty-sixth while I flew to New York.

The night before he left, he and Mamma left me at Tad's house playin' Scrabble while they went down to Antoine's for dinner and to talk "about the future," Mamma said. Mamma got all dressed up and I thought for sure she'd come home with a ring on her finger. Mr. Charbonneau drove me home to the big house and made sure Mr. Patrick was sleeping in his wife's old room like he said he would so I wouldn't be alone. I fell asleep thinking of S-P-E-C-U-L-A-T-I-O-N and E-N-I-G-M-A, H-O-L-L-A-N-D-A-I-S-E and P-R-I-M-O-G-E-N-I-T-U-R-E.

When I woke up in Mrs. Castleberry's bed, the sun was already shining, Mr. Patrick had gone home, and Mamma and Doctor Prout were still wearin' their party clothes and sitting on the veranda. They looked as neat as when they'd started out.

"Morning, Orla," Doctor Prout said.

Mamma smiled up from her chaise lounge.

"It's all arranged," she said.

Doctor Prout poured her coffee in one of Mrs. Castleberry's best china cups.

"Would you like some?" he asked me.

I sat down on a rocker in my pajamas and shook my head no.

"I thought you might like to know that I've decided to open an office down here," Doctor Prout said.

He grinned so both his dimples showed.

My cheeks burned and I felt a cheer in my chest wanting to burst out. But I kept still. Looked over at Mamma. She smiled, too.

Doctor Prout continued.

"Tad's father is preparing the papers. He tells me I can buy your mother's house, which I'll remodel for my office."

I thought of the library room as a waiting room, our kitchen full of cotton swabs and iodine. An examining table where the hutch stood. Sick people where I used to play.

The mail truck stopped outside the fence and Mr. Holden waved like always before stuffing a couple of envelopes and a magazine into the mailbox.

"But you'll live here?" I asked.

Mamma looked at him and waited till he was ready to speak again. But he stretched his arm towards her.

"He'll live there, too."

Why? I wanted to ask, but nothing came out of my mouth. I stared at the floor.

Mamma stood up, came over and took my hands in hers.

"And if, after a year, we all three have gotten to know each other well enough to decide that Prout and I should get married, well, that's when we will."

I slumped in my seat.

This was horrible. Everybody would already know he was my father. People like Mrs. Allaire and Mrs. Haldecott would be talking about me, calling Mamma a trollop.

My lower lip trembled.

"Come on," Mamma said, "let's have breakfast."

She pulled me off the chair. I didn't smile or say anything.

Inside, she and Doctor Prout acted like nothing was wrong. She made French toast, had Doctor Prout crackin' and beating the eggs. I hardly ate a thing. Time we all got cleaned up and dressed, Earl Sharp was pulling into the drive to take Doctor Prout to the airport.

Mamma's eyes filled up when he took her hand, but she tried to joke.

"Don't forget where you live," she said.

Her hands trembled.

"I just about had," he said, and kissed the side of her neck.

Mamma turned and wiped her eyes with her apron.

Then Doctor Prout knelt on one knee in the dust so he and I were eye to eye.

He took a card out of his breast pocket said:

Prout Castleberry, M. D.,
Emergency Medicine,
Massachusetts General Hospital.

"Call anytime you want to."

There was the hospital phone number and he had written in two more, "One for the apartment and the other the coffee shop where Carmine always knows where I am," he said.

"I'll see you in a few weeks," he kissed me on both cheeks.

I looked at him, trying not to sniffle. Turned his mother's ring on my finger.

He moved to stand up, but I held onto his shoulders.

"You'd better not be lying," I said.

My voice sounded crackly as Tad's.

"Cross my heart," he said, and stood up.

He picked his doctor's bag up off the ground while Earl Sharp tipped his chauffeur's hat to Mamma and me and opened the car door.

I turned to Mamma. She took my hand in hers. Then, as the car eased out the drive, I let go to follow beside it, catching up to Doctor Prout's open window. He leaned out, blew me a kiss. The car moved faster. I ran to keep up.

"Doctor P," I yelled, "Doctor P for Père."

Last thing I remember was our fingers touching.

Chapter Thirty-Seven

Lizzy and her mamma, Mrs. Charbonneau and Tad, and Mrs. Makepeace and Spencer had all come up to the Castleberry place for a picnic lunch. Tad's mamma brought a lemon meringue pie, and Mrs. Makepeace was showin' Mrs. Crowther how to crochet lace into snoods that held a lady's hair in place. She was wearin' one herself.

"Mrs. Castleberry sold ten to the manager at Brennan's," she said, while Mrs. Crowther watched her work the crochet needles.

"She told me he had the women in the kitchen wearing them. That they made for a uniform and gracious look."

Mamma had asked Mrs. Crowther to join the group that was planning to meet once a week to make collars, cuffs, snoods, and blouses. Mamma wanted to make bridal gowns and christening outfits, too.

"Big ticket items, like Yvette suggested," she said.

Mamma had invited Mrs. Cowles, too, but, "Bridget told me her husband is planning to drive her and the children to Jesuit Bend to stay with her brother for a few days."

I had seen Denny dragging a big suitcase along the path by their place when I went down to the grocery for Mamma earlier. The *Times Picayune* truck was parked empty in the driveway, must have been between the morning and evening editions. A good thing, too, between the suitcase and the inner tubes, a cooler, and some grocery bags Denny and his daddy lugged from the house to the truck.

"Have a good time," I had hollered over.

Mr. Cowles didn't look up.

Mrs. Cowles came out of the house with a covered dish smelled like cinnamon, walked right over to me.

"Tell your mother I'll miss seeing her," Mrs. Cowles said, then softer, like she was telling me a secret. "Don't know why he couldn't wait until the weekend to go visiting, but you know some folks, once they make up their minds."

She turned to look back at her husband a few times, her neck twitchin' like a bird's.

When I got back to the house, Mamma had already set a table on the veranda. Soon as everybody arrived the ladies laid out fabric swatches for the Easels and Lace workshop there.

We kids had eaten our lunch down on the grass and we were playin' Monopoly on the picnic table outside the kitchen. It was hot enough to make our arms wet without even movin' them.

"Let's go swimming," Tad said.

I leaned over the table to him.

"We'll have to go all the way over near Hester's Ridge," I whispered.

He nodded.

No way Mrs. Haldecott would let us use her dock if Spencer was with us, even if she had been friends with Mrs. Castleberry. Now that Cassie Sharp was still recovering from birthing Belle, Mrs. Haldecott was having the darndest time finding full-time help.

"I'm afraid we won't be able to," I heard Mamma tell her on the telephone. "Yes, they'll be here before the end of the month and staying through August."

Saw Mrs. Haldecott in church on Sunday, I couldn't get her to answer my good morning even though I said it three times. She just looked past me.

Mamma found all the oldest towels she didn't care if they got torn. Handed Tad a big plastic bag full of cookies, too.

"Stay together," Mrs. Makepeace said when we left, "You hear me, Spencer?"

Took us close to an hour to get where we wanted to. We hadn't been swimming but a short time when smoke began billowing in grey-black puffs over the trees. Lizzy and I were already sunning ourselves on one of the towels eating the cookies. Tad and Spencer raced over and over from one rock to another, Tad giving Spencer a three-kick head start because he was four years younger.

"Where's the fire?" I asked nobody in particular.

Then we heard the siren. Three blasts, stop. Three blasts again.

"The Hollow," Tad said.

We all stopped moving and listened again. More blasts, then the fire truck siren winding itself into a wail.

The smoke rolled gracefully above the trees, darkening their greens with its shadow.

"I'm going to see what happened," said Tad. "You take Spencer and Lizzy home."

"No," I said. "I'm coming, too."

Lizzy was tying her sneakers.

"My mamma finds out I left you, she'll tan my hide," said Spencer.

Lizzy stood by me, holding the cookie bag half full now.

"I don't want to go to The Hollow," she said. "I might run into the boogey-man."

I gave her a look said "stupid," Spencer standing not two feet away from her.

Tad was already looking down river, making a plan.

Lizzy swung the cookie bag between her legs. The siren screamed closer through the trees.

"Tell you what. Everybody follow me; then, if you want, you can wait where I'll show you, somewhere no one will see you."

Single-file, we hugged the river away from town, then crossed over the narrowest part, where a small peninsula jutted out into the water and somebody had built a rickety walk-bridge to the other bank.

"Hold the ropes," Tad said, like he needed to tell us.

He led us across to a path almost invisible, so overgrown it was with weeds and fallen branches. It led to the old box factory. Nothing but a faded cement building with its roof caved in and what used to be a parking lot grown weedy and cracked, right where the paved road turned gravel on its way to The Hollow.

We stopped to wipe our faces, followed the smoke, ran now towards it.

"This way," Tad pointed.

Lizzy paused.

"Mamma wouldn't like it if I went in there," she said.

Tad and I looked at her, then at each other, then back at her again.

"Then either set yourself down on one of the towels behind the factory or follow the paved road back to town," I said and pointed.

She looked both ways, but didn't move.

The air was blackening. Tad and I started for The Hollow, Spencer right behind. We hadn't gone very far into the tunnel the trees made when Lizzy yelled, "Wait!" and left her bag and towel to follow.

The smoke burned the inside of my nose. Lizzy coughed. At first, we could walk four abreast, but when the road narrowed, Tad and I went ahead.

"Come on," he said, and the both of us walked fast and faster toward the fire.

"Wait," Lizzy said, running ahead and grabbing me back of my blouse.

"I'm scared," she whined.

I turned, pushed her hand off me. Spencer took it and she let him.

The air was dirty with ashes. I heard nothing except the whir of the fire engine's motor. The birds had disappeared and no insects were buzzing.

"Let's go back," Lizzy said.

She had let go Spencer's hand and was crying.

I turned around and pinched her arm.

"Stop it," I said, "just stop bein' a baby."

She pushed me away, slapped at my hand.

"You think you can boss me because you're rich now," she said. "Just like my mamma told me, you'd get too big for your britches."

I wanted to pinch her again. But what if it was true?

I looked back for Tad, but he had already gone ahead and I didn't want to lose him.

"Listen," I took Lizzy's hands in mine. "I'm scared, too," I said, "but I've got to see what's going on."

I pulled her beside me and we continued on. Spencer walked behind us alone.

When we reached the opening of trees, Tad motioned for Lizzy and Spencer to hide themselves in the thicket at the right. Then I ran to him so we could both crouch behind a hedgerow at the left.

The fire engine took up the center of the circle of cabins. The air hung leaden and murky. Water from the fire hose attached to the water tank on the truck sprayed what had been the Sharp cabin. What I could see around the fire truck looked to be a pile of burned, smoldering timber. No roof left at all.

"Listen," I whispered to Tad.

A group of Negro women knelt in a row not too far from where Lizzy and Spencer hid, swayin' over something I couldn't see, singing a mournful song.

"*O Lord, dast bring her home,*
Her home, O Lord, Sweet Home," they sang.

Tad stood up, tryin' to see over them. "Somebody died," he said. "Listen to the words."

One of the firemen sometimes came to Sam's walked around to our side of the engine and threw his rubber jacket up into the cab. Vernon, I think his name was. He played baseball with some boys lived near the Allaire's when they were off work. Lizzy and I sometimes saw them at the park.

"Two less niggers to worry about," he said to another fireman.

The other fireman lit a cigarette and offered Vernon one, too.

Vernon shook his head no, so the other fireman lit his, dropped the match and rubbed it into the ground with his boot, took a puff, then said, "Have a little compassion, Vern. Even if they are niggers, nobody wants to see a mother and her dead kid."

"No!" I screamed.

I felt myself running before I thought to.

The singing women turned and tried to hold me, to keep me back, but I kicked and kicked till they let go. Other side of them on the ground in front of me, kneeling, was the magic lady. Her eyes were closed, her hands outstretched, and she was swaying over two bodies covered in sheets. One was small as a doll. And what used to be, must have been Cassie Sharp's feet stuck out, seared from the flames, broiled beyond imagining.

My mouth opened, but no sound came out. My eyes stared, unblinking. I felt my brain trying to believe what I saw. My lips found my tongue. I listened. Waited. My feet felt nailed to the ground. Someone came up from behind me. Hand I knew was Tad's clamped onto my arm.

The women had stopped singing. The magic lady opened her eyes and got up, one leg moving at a time, her hands pressed on the ground to push herself to standing. She walked around the bodies slow, her own procession, till she stood right in front of me.

"Now, child," she said.

Her voice was a giant turtle crossing a wide road.

"You go on home. No place for you to be here now."

She nodded to Tad to let go. He dropped his arm. Then she turned me around by my shoulders. Walked me over to the fire truck. Tad put out his hand for me to take and motioned for me to climb up into the cab.

"Jesus," said Vernon, "what do you kids want to be hanging around niggers for?"

The magic lady didn't budge. Bore her eyes into Vernon's till he looked away. I felt too heavy to move.

Lizzy stood up from the thicket, came out, and ran to him. She smiled. He patted her on the head, then jumped into the cab to make room on the seat, came back down, and walked around to the other side of the truck.

I looked at Spencer standing by the thicket all alone. Then back at the women. One of them went over to him and took him by the hand.

"Afternoon, Miss Bertha," he said.

"Your parents will be worried," she said, and brought him over with the others.

I sucked in air, but it only made me cough. Then I looked up at the magic lady's face. It was still.

"Magic," I whispered, my voice cracking, "you were supposed to do magic."

She took my hands, drew them to her face.

"Look here," she said.

My fingers felt her skin. Lines of grooves around her mouth. Creases. Furrows of brown. Her eyes the only light.

"Old," she said, "that is my magic."

The women moved again, circling Cassie and Belle once more, this time Spencer with them. He knew the words to their song.

The magic lady continued.

"Lasting," she said, "that is my only trick. See everything, look at the sorry way folks is, and still get up every day and make some soup, feed somebody besides yourself."

She placed her hands on my shoulders, pressed down, molded her fingers to me.

"What you make, Orla, what you going to make, that be your magic."

She lifted her hands off. I didn't want her to let go.

Vernon came back around.

"Get in," he said, and helped Lizzy up into the cab.

251

I looked at Tad. He stared back. No words needed. "Come on, then," he said finally, and eased me up onto the fire truck.

The other fireman drove, pushing the truck through the trees, ripping some branches as we went. Tad and I stood on the side of the truck, ducking now and again and closing our eyes, gripping the hot metal, one of Tad's hands on mine, making sure I didn't let go.

I looked back just when the dirt road changed to gravel. The circle of women and Spencer still swayed left and right, their song getting fainter and fainter. The magic lady, her hand raised once in good-bye. The black smoke turning into a dark cloud behind us. The fire bell clanging once, twice, once more, then done.

There was nothin' I could do.

I felt so tired.

The fire truck ran smooth now over cement. Passed by the park where couple of little kids ran to the edge of the street and waved.

I looked away from them, down at the ground beneath us, grateful for Tad's hand on mine.

Time we rode into St. Suplice, folks had gathered at Sam's, the way they always did when the fire truck pulled into the garage just back of the fish shack.

Somebody yelled, "Look, they're carrying kids."

All I remember was getting into Mr. Charbonneau's car.

"Now, then," he said real soft and close to my ear, "you sit right beside me, Orla, and we'll get you to your mother."

He drove slow. His red convertible might as well have been a hearse.

We passed our little house. Seemed a long time ago.

"Son," he turned to the back seat to talk to Tad, "whatever possessed you to bring children there?"

But before Tad could explain, Reverend Makepeace pulled alongside from the other direction with his wife. He looked to the back seat.

"Where is Spencer?" he asked.

I looked across to him. His face was stern.

"In The Hollow," Tad said.

Mr. Charbonneau turned in his seat. "You mean you left him!" He sounded angry.

I looked away.

"Thank God," Reverend Makepeace said. "He's safe there."

Mr. Charbonneau took a cigar out of the ashtray and bit into it. I knew Tad would be in trouble when they got home.

Reverend Makepeace drove off and, before I could make myself feel invisible, Mr. Charbonneau pulled into the Castleberry driveway.

Mamma looked surprised to see us.

"Did you have a good time?" she asked on her way down from the veranda.

Then she saw me.

"Orla," she said, and knelt by the car door.

But I pushed the door open and ran past her inside and up the two flights of stairs.

The attic was hot. I lay myself down between Baby Jesus and Gabriel broken. I breathed slow, motionless, tried to become a statue, too. Wanted my mind to shut down. To forget. To become as small and dark as possible. I closed my eyes.

Something creaked. I tried to see, blinked a few times till I realized it was black night. I turned on my side, my back sore from the floor so hard. Mamma was asleep beside me. I stared at her back till I fell asleep again.

When the sun woke me she had already gone downstairs. Heard her in the kitchen. She didn't come find me or bother me about breakfast or try to have me talk. I went outside, dropped myself onto one of the chaise lounges and saw my easel set up in the yard where there'd be shade most of the morning.

Time the milk truck passed on its way to the Haldecott place, I was sitting in front of the easel, my brush thickening the canvas with blackened orange, bruised purple. I wrapped little Belle in a sorrowful yellow sheet should have been white. I used the smallest brush. The most delicate. Like I was stroking her arm singing her a lullaby.

Chapter Thirty-Eight

Time Doctor Prout returned to St. Suplice, Mr. Cowles had been moved from the hospital at Convent over to the paraplegic ward at Veterans' Hospital near the Capitol. He'd been run off the highway by a trooper got word he was wanted for questioning, and he'd tried to run. The trooper's bullet cost him the use of both his legs. Tad's daddy was trying to find a way for Mrs. Cowles to keep the house for Katie and Denny. Fire chief determined the cause of the fire to be copies of *The Times Picayune* dipped in kerosene, set aflame, and thrown into the Sharp cabin. Mr. Owens had been the one to tell Earl Sharp the news. Reverend and Mrs. Makepeace had taken Mr. Sharp in. Mr. Owens said he could start driving again anytime he was ready to.

So it was Mr. Patrick who met Doctor Prout at the airport instead and brought him home again.

"Are you packed?" he asked me soon as I ran out to meet him.

I was. Excited and nervous, too.

"And you," Mamma said, wearin' shoes like Tante Yvette's, "eager to meet Gabriella?"

We started into the house together.

"Ready or not," he said.

Morning dawned blue and unusually dry. I changed my clothes three times, finally settling on my striped seersucker jumper. Mamma had let me shave my legs for the first time, and I rubbed lotion that smelled like citrus on them so the scratches wouldn't show. My flight was scheduled to leave at 8:35. Gabriella would disembark at noon.

"Let's go," Doctor Prout said.

He drove himself, him, Mamma, and me squished in the front seat together a little after six.

The airport was crowded. Men mostly in business suits and some ladies wearin' hats and white gloves stood in line ahead of us. I saw a baby carriage, too, but mosquito netting covered it so I didn't see the child inside.

At the departures desk, the attendant pinned a paper full of information on my dress like I was a piece of cargo. I'd be sitting up front with one of the stewardesses, who would stay right with me in New York until Tante Yvette picked me up.

While Mamma and me made sure the twenty dollars was in the wallet Mr. Patrick had given me as a bon voyage present, Doctor Prout spoke to the desk clerk. Her name tag read Bonnie right above the pin she wore in the shape of wings.

"Thanks," he said, just as the loudspeaker boomed.

"Flight 682 for New York's Idlewild Airport, now departing from Gate 4," a man's voice announced.

Doctor Prout carried my overnight bag Mamma borrowed from Mrs. Castleberry's luggage armoire, and Mamma took my hand. Together we rushed to the gate.

The attendant at the door checked the information on my ticket against the tag on my jumper, smiled, and nodded for me to pass.

I didn't move. I had never gone anywhere but the grocery or church alone.

"You're all set," she said.

She spoke in a sing-song voice and her cheeks plumped when she smiled.

I turned from her to Mamma and Doctor Prout. They stood side by side. Doctor Prout stooped and kissed me on the top of my head.

Mamma threw her arms around me and said, "Have the best time you can."

I tried to turn my quivering lips into a smile, felt like I wanted to run to the plane and never move at the same time.

"Last call for Flight 682," said the voice on the loudspeaker.

The attendant tapped my shoulder.

"Let's go," she said, and pointed to a glass door.

Together Mamma and Doctor Prout gave me a little push. The attendant waved.

"Have a good flight," she said.

A man with a briefcase stopped to let me go ahead of him. Gave a nod to Mamma.

"First time?" he asked.

"Yes," Mamma said, her voice full of how she loved me.

I breathed deep, stood up tall, felt my legs begin to move. Hoisted Mrs. Castleberry's bag onto my shoulder the way Tante Yvette held hers.

The sun blazed through the windows on both sides of the passageway. The door at the end opened onto the tarmac. I took my place in line and followed the other passengers. We crossed to the plane and climbed up the stairs. At the top of the steps I turned to look back. But there wasn't time.

"Welcome aboard," the pilot said.

He tipped his hat, looked at my tag, and pointed me towards my seat right up front.

An older lady was already sitting down. She got up to let me have the window seat that matched my ticket.

"I'm off to see my new grandson," she said, and showed me how to fasten the seatbelt. "How about you?"

But a stewardess interrupted, "Would you mind putting your seat into the upright position, Ma'am, until we reach cruising level?"

I looked out the window and saw Mamma and Doctor Prout by the glass wall inside the terminal.

Before long, the engines rumbled beneath me and the stewardesses walked up and down the aisle helpin' everyone get settled. The plane was crowded and a baby way back toward the tail began to cry.

"Good morning, ladies and gentlemen."

The pilot's voice sounded warm and friendly.

"We sure are glad to have you aboard our flight to New York's Idlewild Airport. The weather there is a comfortable seventy-five degrees today, and we should have you landed in time for lunch in the big city."

I had told Tante Yvette I wanted to try Chinese food. Mr. Patrick made a face when he heard me, then said, "See if you can bring me some chopsticks. I'll use them to train my plantings."

The pilot continued. "We'd like to welcome a special guest aboard today."

I looked around, wondered if I was going to meet somebody famous.

"Ladies and gentlemen, aboard our flight this morning is one of Louisiana's own, Miss Orla Gwen Gleason, recently named a promising young artist of America."

My face burned. Goosebumps popped up all over my shiny legs. People looked around in their seats.

"Where is she sitting?" the lady next to me asked.

"Her paintings are displayed in The Metropolitan Museum of Art even as we speak," the pilot said.

Seemed everyone but me burst into applause while I scrunched down in my seat.

"Why, you're her," the lady next to me said. "Here she is."

She waved her hand, then pointed down at me. My face burned.

"Well, I'll be. Wait until I tell my daughter."

The engines hummed, then growled beneath us.

"Stewardesses, take your seats," the pilot said.

The plane began to move. I squinted out the window at the terminal and saw Mamma and Doctor Prout waving. I waved back, knowing they couldn't see me and knowing it didn't matter. I watched as long as I could, craning my neck till my head pressed the glass. Then the plane turned sharp onto the runway.

"We're off," a man behind me said.

I gripped the seat cushion and bit my lip. My whole body was shaking.

Fast and faster, thrusting forward, we were rushing, skimming the ground, big tires rolling and rolling. A roar. And then, like magic, we lifted up, felt light, felt like floating, a ferris wheel feel.

My head fell back on the headrest. The plane aimed high, raised itself above cement and swamp, buildings and water. Banking, turning, up and up we soared. My ears popped, so I swallowed again and again.

I looked down and back, saw New Orleans get small. Watched parcels of green reach out on the water like arms. Gazed at fields golden and brown, clover and orange. Then came the clouds, billowing, holding us in until, burst, we were through to the heavenly sky.

It took most an hour for me to calm down by Doctor Prout's watch on my wrist. He had added a hole on the leather strap to make it fit me tight enough. My seatmate had fallen asleep and she snored. I pushed my seat back, too, and, like her, closed my eyes.

Nothing 'cept everything had changed.

I took a deep breath. Then another. Knew how important each one was. That a body never knew how many she'd have left.

The plane swooped around and I sat up to see. Big sky. No edges. Sun and clouds both.

This is my life now. Beginning again, alone and aloft in the sky.

I feel my heart beat, know my brushes are ready. I flex my fingers and blink into the light.

I'll look at everything, no matter what, paint more and more till I need a whole barn for my murals not yet begun.

Gabriella wrote Doctor Prout that the Contessa is coming for Christmas.

Before she arrives, I'll go up to the attic and bring down the gesso statues. Mamma will set up the crèche on the veranda. Doctor Prout will hang the white lights. Gabriella will come down from The Julliard, maybe with Tante Yvette. We'll decorate the tree, and everyone will talk at once. Mamma will invite Reverend and Mrs. Makepeace and Spencer for eggnog. Earl Sharp, too, if he feels up to it. Sam will take pictures. The phone will ring, and Doctor Prout and I will go out to stitch up a leg or birth another baby. More people will die. Mrs. Cowles will wear a brave face in spite of her sorrowful heart. The house will smell of cinnamon and roast beef.

We'll hear tires in the driveway. We'll run outside. Gabriella will help her mother out of the car. There will hugging and kissing and languages and tears.

"Guarde, look, Contessa," I'll say.

I'll point to the manger and the Angel Gabriel we glued back together.

"They're all here," I'll tell her. "Mrs. Castleberry kept them all."

THE END

Acknowledgements

This book came to fruition in Rachel Basch's novel workshops, and to her I owe a debt of gratitude for her mentoring and her example. Chantel Acevedo, Jeanne Archambault, James Benn, Marie Clark, Bill Holder, Francine Knight, Sari Rosenblatt, and Carole Snyder share my sincere thanks for their careful reading, re-reading, and critical insights regarding the original manuscript.

My thanks to Wesleyan University Writers' Conference for awarding me a scholarship that supported my work and provided both quiet spaces to draft as well as a community of writers to join. Additional and greatly appreciated funding was provided by the Hartford Council for the Arts Beatrice Fox Auerbach Foundation and the Nigel Taplin Innovative Teaching grants.

To novelist Louis Bayard and fellow members of his historical writing workshop at Yale University, my gratitude for a helpful and delightful week spent improving craft.

Julia Pistell, Director of Writing Programs at Mark Twain House, Hartford, Connecticut, continues to be a tireless advocate.

Continued thanks to all my colleagues and the families of Chase Collegiate School, Waterbury, Connecticut, for your generous and unwavering support and encouragement. In particular, for your patience and wise counsel: Polly Peterson, Joe and Leslie Hadam, Kyle and Pam Kahuda, Nedra and Rich Gusenburg, Tim Watt and Amity Gaige, Bob and Liz Cutrofello, Gus Haracopos, Carol and Pete Riebe,

Irene Belden, Helen Drake. To my students especially, it is a privilege to share my days with you.

Thanks to Kristen Baclawski, Matt South, Robin Masiewicz, Tom McDade, Frank and Ruth Steponaitis, Dan and Joyce D'Alessio, Barbara and Phil Benevento, Marion and Robert Bradley, Terry and Chris Dannen, Elaine Muldowney, Barbara Ruggiero and David Whitehouse, Rena Shove, Anna Shove, Nina and Gorgen Gostas, Steve Parlato, Janet Parlato, Garrard Conley, Diana Smith, Tracey O'Shaughnessy, Tom Santopietro, Linda and Dan Sloan, Joanna Clapps Herman, Iris Romeo, and book club friends Mike and Pam Hull, Patricia and John Philip, Suzanne Noel and Jim Wigren, Sharon and Dan Wilson. Extended thanks also to the Fabry, Cohen, and Plasko families; the Petlock, Horny, Kane, Ohrin, Janoski, and Swatkoski families; the Pelosi, Ciampi, and D'Avino families of Frigento, Italy; and to Crupi, Pesino, Chiucarello, and Giordano cousins.

Michael James, Chris Paige, Midori Snyder, Christine Horner, and Danielle Boschert at Penmore Press—thank you for giving this book a wonderful home.

Fran and Maureen Donnarumma, Teresa and Ed Wasil, Mike and Ellen Donnarumma; nieces and nephews Alessandra, Egon, Caroline, Colin Donnarumma; Emily and Ethan Wasil; George and Erin Donnarumma—how fortunate to know your love.

Louise and the late Carmen Donnarumma, thank you for teaching me to love the written word.

Veronica and Robert Sharnick, thank you for your loving acceptance and support.

Wayne Sharnick: "Love consists in this, that two solitudes protect and touch and greet each other." (Rainer Maria Rilke). As ever, yours.

ABOUT THE AUTHOR

MARY DONNARUMMA SHARNICK

Mary Donnarumma Sharnick has been writing ever since the day she printed her long name on her first library card.

A native of Connecticut, she graduated from Fairfield University with a degree in English and earned a master's degree from Trinity College, Hartford. She has been awarded a scholarship from Wesleyan Writers' Conference (2008), two Nigel Taplin Innovative Teaching grants (2008, 2011), and a fellowship from the Hartford Council for the Arts Beatrice Fox Auerbach Foundation (2010). A student of novelists Rachel Basch and Louis Bayard, Mary has participated in the 2014 Yale Writers' Conference historical fiction workshop and has presented at Auburn University's

Writers' Conference (2012), the Association for Writers and Writing Programs conference in Boston (2013), the Italian American Historical Association's conference in Toronto (2014), and annually at the Mark Twain Writers' Conference in Hartford, as well as at the University of Connecticut's Osher Lifelong Learning Institute, Waterbury, CT. Her research has taken her to Venice, Italy, the Deep South, and monastic communities in Italy, Vermont, and Connecticut.

Mary's first two novels, *Thirst (2012)* and *Plagued (2014)*, are set in the Venetian lagoon during the seventeenth and fifteenth centuries, respectively. *Thirst* is being adapted for the operatic stage by composer Gerard Chiusano and librettists Mary Chiusano and Robert Cutrofello.

Orla's Canvas, Mary's first book with Penmore Press, is a coming-of-age tale about a young artist set against the backdrop of Civil Rights-era New Orleans.

At present, Mary is drafting a novel-in-stories set in both America and abroad.

Mary reviews books for the *New York Journal of Books, Southern Humanities Review, America*, and other journals. Excerpts of her memoir-in-progress have appeared in the *American Journal of Alzheimer's Disease and Related Dementias, Italian Americana*, and *Healing Ministry*, among others. Her short story, "The Rule," appeared in *Voices in Italian Americana*.

Chair of the English Department and writing instructor at Chase Collegiate School, Waterbury, CT, Mary leads her writing students on slow travel tours of Italy, the country she considers her second home.

Please visit www.marydonnarummasharnick.com for more information, updates, and to contact Mary.

———————

If You Enjoyed This Book

Please place a review as this helps the author
and visit the website of

PENMORE PRESS
www.penmorepress.com

All Penmore Press books are available directly through our website, as well as Amazon.com, Barnes and Noble and Nook, Sony Reader, Apple iTunes, Kobo books and via bookshops across the United States, Canada, the UK, Australia and Europe.

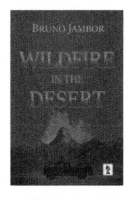

WILDFIRE IN THE DESERT

BY

BRUNO JAMBOR

Action Adventure, Crime, Mystery,
Southwest History

Highly entertaining, well researched and original:

A Navy veteran returns home to his ancestral land to escape the pace of modern life. His nephew begs him to hide the drugs he is transporting to escape his pursuers.

An astronomer trying to find a replacement for his estranged wife finds solace in his work with the stars.

Police and the drug cartel try to recover the missing shipment, regardless of consequences, ready to sacrifice any opponent.

The antagonists crisscross the desert of Southern Arizona in a chess game where the loser will be eliminated.

Unexpected help comes from a famous missionary who blazed new paths through the same desert three centuries ago.

The climactic resolution will captivate readers of this thriller with deep spiritual undertones.

PENMORE PRESS
www.penmorepress.com

Historical fiction and nonfiction
Paperback available for order on line
and as Ebook with all major distributers

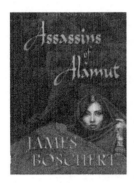

ASSASSINS OF ALAMUT
BY
JAMES BOSCHERT

An Epic Novel of Persia and Palestine in the Time of the Crusades

The Assassins of Alamut is a riveting tale, painted on the vast canvas of life in Palestine and Persia during the 12th century.

On one hand, it's a tale of the crusades—as told from the Islamic side—where Shi'a and Sunni are as intent on killing Ismaili Muslims as crusaders. In self-defense, the Ismailis develop an elite band of highly trained killers called Hashshashin whose missions are launched from their mountain fortress of Alamut.

But it's also the story of a French boy, Talon, captured and forced into the alien world of the assassins. Forbidden love for a princess is intertwined with sinister plots and self-sacrifice, as the hero and his two companions discover treachery and then attempt to evade the ruthless assassins of Alamut who are sent to hunt them down.

It's a sweeping saga that takes you over vast snow-covered mountains, through the frozen wastes of the winter plateau, and into the fabulous cites of Hamadan, Isfahan, and the Kingdom of Jerusalem.

"A brilliant first novel, worthy of Bernard Cornwell at his best."—Tom Grundner

PENMORE PRESS
www.penmorepress.com

Historical fiction and nonfiction
Paperback available for order on line
and as Ebook with all major distributers

THE LAUNDRY ROOM

BY

LYNDA LIPPMAN-LOCKHART

The Laundry Room dramatizes a fascinating moment in the history of the founding of Israel as a self-ruling nation. Based on actual events, Lynda Lippmann-Lockhart follows the lives of several young Israelis as they found a kibbutz and run a clandestine ammunition factory, which supplied Israeli troops fighting against Arab forces following the end of British occupation in the late 1940s. Under British rule, it was illegal for Israelis to possess firearms, so it was necessary not only to create and stockpile bullets for the coming war, but to do so in secret.

The ingenuity, courage, and sheer audacity displayed by the members of the code-named "Ayalon Institute" as they operated their factory right under the noses of the British military make for an intriguing tale. Lippmann-Lockhart shows readers what it might have been like to be one of the young pioneers whose work shaped the outcome of Israel's fight for independence. The Ayalon Institute remains standing to this day, but the secret hidden under the kibbutz's laundry room was not revealed until the 1970s. It was made a National Historic Site in 1987 and is open to the public every day of the year except Yom Kippur.

FENMORE PRESS
www.fenmorepress.com

Historical fiction and nonfiction
Paperback available for order on line
and as Ebook with all major distributers

Penmore Press
Challenging, Intriguing, Adventurous, Historical and Imaginative

www.penmorepress.com

CPSIA information can be obtained at www.ICGtesting.com
Printed in the USA
BVOW06s1807061015

420683BV00003B/3/P